Letting Go of your Bananas

*12 Keys on How You Can
Become More Successful by
Getting Rid of Everything
Rotten in Your Life*

Letting Go
of your
Bananas

*12 Keys on How You Can
Become More Successful by
Getting Rid of Everything
Rotten in Your Life*

By
DR. DANIEL T. DRUBIN

Author of
BUSTING YOUR RUT

Published by 4th Dimension Management Corporation

Also by Dr. Daniel T. Drubin

Busting Your Rut

To find out more about having Danny Drubin speak at your convention or work with your company, please contact:

4th Dimension Management Corporation
1363 W. Stony Run Place
Oro Valley, AZ 85737
(520) 575-0207

Website: www.masterofchange.net
E-mail: change@xmission.com

First edition

Cover Design: Ragont Design
Book Layout: Michelle VanGeest
Printed by Dickinson Press Inc.

Library of Congress Cataloging-in-Publication Data has been applied for.

ISBN 0-9708559-1-5

2 3 4 5 6 7 8 9 10
Printed in the United States

Dedication

For Laura, my partner in life and in business…
Everyone was right. I am the world's luckiest man! You have
helped shape me into more than I ever hoped that I could
become. All I ever did was build businesses; however, you took
on a much bigger project, and you built me!

To my children Peter and Jennifer…
Your love and support drives my life. I love you for all that you
are and all that you will become.

Acknowledgements

This book could not have been written without the values instilled in me by my mom and dad. Though you are no longer with me in the traditional sense, I feel your presence and hear your words. The wisdom you imparted to me resonates in my mind every day.

To my sister Cyndy. Your love and support is a constant reminder of just how important family is.

To Jimmie and Jenny Vassalotti for indulging me and allowing me to spend part of our vacation to complete this book. Your love and friendship keep me smiling and always make me aware that life is supposed to be fun.

To Dr. Larry Markson for providing me with a stage upon which I was able to learn, grow and advance my knowledge and skills.

Foreword

By Peter J. Drubin

People often ask me what it is like being Danny's son. Their questions are partially out of curiosity but mostly because they are interested in just how much of what he teaches he incorporates into his own life, and how much I have been exposed to growing up in a world of positive thinking and motivational messages.

As early as I can remember, I was encouraged to write goals for myself, think the very best of myself, save money and find the good in other people. And, while as a kid some of the things that I was asked to do made very little sense, I can now see the wisdom and value in going through life with a plan and a positive attitude.

The message contained in *Letting Go of Your Bananas* is an absolute reflection of how we operate our business and how Danny lives his life. When I was fourteen years old, my mom and dad decided to move with my sister Jen and me from our home on Long Island, New York to Park City, Utah. In doing so, Danny left his business, his family and friends in search of a different life experience. On numerous occasions I have seen his willingness to let go of his existing comfort and explore what is possible beyond the known and the obvious.

In *Letting Go of Your Bananas*, Danny will share with you his 12 Keys to a richer and more rewarding life, a life filled with limitless possibilities and personal freedom.

Fearless in his ability to change easily and often, Danny now resides in Tucson, Arizona, where he works with his clients from around the world and continues to improve a golf game that is at its best erratic and at its worst pure comedy.

The progression to perfection begins by letting go of the ordinary and focusing on a clear vision of what you see your future to be.

Contents

12 Keys on How to Get Rid of Everything Rotten in Your Life

Everyone Has A Story

L ife is like a bunch of bananas—some good and some
rotten. *Letting Go of Your Bananas* is a book that will
help you identify the areas, situations, circumstances
and people in your life that you need to let go of. They represent the bananas that you are better off without. At the same
time you can select all of the positive bananas in your bunch
and enjoy the sweetness that they add to your life.

We each have a bunch of bananas, and each rotting banana in our bunch represents an area in our life where we are
limited, settling or just plain stuck. Perhaps we are stuck with
old behaviors or false beliefs. Maybe our obstacles are very
real or just vividly imagined. The bananas we hold onto may
be of our own doing or thrust upon us by others. What matters most is that each of us clings to some things that prevent
us from getting some of the things that we want most in our
lives. This book is about your personal bunch of bananas,
and the things that you hold onto and the things that hold
you back and limit your life. Consider the following: at the
very moment you decide to let go of your bananas and move

beyond the barriers that hold you back, you can live the life of your dreams.

The more people I meet, the more intrigued I become with how many ways people can overcome the obstacles that are in the way of getting what they want. I do believe that each of us has a unique destiny, a special reason why we were put here, a mission to fulfill and a grand purpose for our existence. *Letting Go of Your Bananas* was created so you can free yourself of the obstacles that hold you back and allow you to find a life free of rotten bananas, a life of personal freedom and a life of unlimited potential.

Everyone has a story. And each of our stories seems to perfectly explain our existence and our present condition in life. Have you ever wondered what series of coincidences and events brought you to the place where you find yourself right now? Have you ever stopped to consider that the universe has a grand design for you? There is one, you know, a grand design for you. At this very moment you are exactly where you are supposed to be, doing those things that you are supposed to be doing, like reading this book. While you may not be able to alter all of the events of your past that bring you to where you are right now, the message in *Letting Go Of Your Bananas* will provide you with an opportunity to write the story of the rest of your life. And, while the story of your past may be interesting, exciting, challenging or just plain depressing, your future has yet to be written. Well, your future begins right now.

I was born in 1946, or as my children call it, the "black and white days," because there are no color photographs of my childhood. However, my story began in April of 1920 when a young Polish immigrant by the name of Rose Altman, already the mother of two, found out that she was pregnant with a child she could not afford to have. Torn with conflicting emotions, she had been told that there was a doctor in New York City who would perform an illegal abortion for a small fee and, as much as the woman did not want to lose her baby, she sought out the doctor's help.

When the day arrived that the abortion was to be performed, the woman traveled from her home to the doctor's office and waited patiently in the doctor's waiting room. Unbeknownst to Rose, the doctor, a married man, had impregnated his employee/nurse who he had promised to marry if she aborted her pregnancy. Well, the nurse did exactly that, believing that the doctor would then leave his wife and marry her. On the day of Rose's abortion, the doctor told his nurse that he had decided to stay with his wife and would not be marrying the nurse. The nurse—obviously shocked and dismayed—left the office, returned with a pistol and shot the doctor to death.

No doctor, no abortion! Rose took this remarkable event as an omen that perhaps she was supposed to have this baby after all, and she left the doctor's office. So, she went home to complete her pregnancy and give birth. This story is true and, for me, extremely fortunate. You see, the young woman, Rose, was my grandmother and the baby she gave birth to was my mother. That's how I got here and that's my story. As a child I was told that I had a special mission in life, a mission to help make people's lives better. And that all of the events of that day in the spring of 1920 brought me to the exact place where I was supposed to be.

You may never know what life events brought you to the place where you find yourself at this very moment. And I am not certain that you need to know or understand how you got to where you are. The only thing that really matters is what you are going to do with the rest of your life. If you are willing to believe that everything you have experienced in your life to this point was designed to allow you to fulfill your destiny of greatness, you are on your way to busting every barrier you encounter and letting go of every rotten banana you may be holding.

The journey we take and the roadblocks we encounter on our way to a more complete life are the very things that shape our character and make us one-of-a-kind people. I believe that you are exactly where you are supposed to be and all of the events that have occurred in your life have been intentionally placed before you to allow you to maximize your human potential and realize your personal greatness.

It has been said that we attract into our lives all of the situations and circumstances that enable us to shape our own destinies. We attract all of our life opportunities as well as all of our personal and professional bananas or barriers. And, while taking advantage of opportunities can make our lives enjoyable and rewarding, busting through personal and professional barriers is the trait of greatness.

A banana is loosely defined as something that you cling to that blocks you from getting from one place to another. When you stop to consider that we spend the majority of our existence getting from one place to another, learning how to rid yourself of limitations is an essential part of creating a life that is both stimulating and challenging.

Becoming a barrier buster and letting go of your limitations demands that you explore all of the options that can improve the quality of all aspects of your life. When it comes to ridding yourself of your real or perceived limitations, your most important weapons will be resourcefulness and urgency. The more you want to go beyond your present place, the more you will be driven to find creative ways to reach your destination.

All success in life is about getting from wherever you are to wherever you want to be. Letting go of your past, where you have come from, and getting to a better future requires that you change the ways you think and behave. Only once you embrace new thoughts and behaviors will you live a life free of rotten bananas. Resourceful barrier busters know that the only thing that matters is the end result, not necessarily how they reach their desired outcome. Their strategy for success is rather simple…over, under, around or through.

People who are committed to living a life free of rotten bananas approach each task with an "I am prepared to do whatever it takes" attitude. All of their actions are consistent with their attitudes of making a better life for themselves. They just believe that they can overcome any barrier with pure will, determination and a burning desire to improve their lives and the lives of others.

To go beyond your present place, you must be driven by a burning desire and mentally fueled by the exciting outcomes that await you. Consider if you will that you are ideally designed to be living the life you presently have. In order for you to let go of your past and create a brighter future, you must be willing to alter your personal design. You alter your personal design and let go of your rotten bananas by asking yourself some high quality questions. Questions like, "What is possible for me?" or "What do I really want out of life?"

Curiosity about your personal and professional potential should become the driving force in your life. Remember, where you are in your present situation is not nearly as important as where you are going in your life. All successful living is about direction, and as long as you consistently move in the direction of your dreams, you are on your way to a life free of the limitations of the past.

If as you begin to read this book you feel stuck, that's okay. How you feel right now is only a temporary situation if you are prepared to break out of your state of stuck and go for barrier-busting change. Your present state of stuck can be totally unimportant in the grand scheme of what life holds in store for you. In fact, it's probably a good idea to consider all that you have gone through to this point in your life as one huge learning experience. All that matters is what you do from this point on. Now can be the beginning of a newer and better life—a life filled with limitless opportunities and amazing experiences. After all, that's what you were destined for at birth, yearned for in your youth and crave as an adult.

Letting Go of Your Bananas provides you with 12 keys that you need to know and adhere to in order to take you from wherever you are to wherever you want to be. The choice is yours and to the degree that you adhere to these 12 keys and make them part of your life, you will alter your destiny.

This is the time for you to learn and grow. This is the time to begin your personal journey of improvement. This is the time to sort out the bunch of bananas that represents your life. This is the time to keep the bananas that fulfill and enrich your life and get rid of every rotten banana that holds you back.

Letting Go of Your Bananas

All barrier busting and personal growth begins the moment you are willing to accept the truth about yourself. And the truth is, most of your bananas or limitations, whether real or imagined, have either been created by you or someone important in your life. So much of what we become in our lives has a great deal to do with the people and beliefs that we were exposed to as children. Children tend to be wide open to suggestion and to modeling the behaviors of those around them to the point where they sometimes take on the characteristics of people who influence their lives. Without an effective way to filter out some of the things they are exposed to—some of which may not be in their ultimate best interest—they become pre-programmed to think and act a certain way. The good news is that regardless of what you may have been exposed to early on, or for that matter later in your life, you can change your life by using your free will and power of choice.

You get to decide right now if you want to continue on your present path of life and have those obstacles keep you where you are, or do whatever is necessary to go beyond those barriers. You decide which of the bananas in your bunch are worth keeping and which of the rotten bananas you want to rid yourself of.

I have been told that the way they used to capture monkeys in Africa was by placing bananas in the bottoms of narrow neck jars. When a monkey came upon the jar, in an effort to remove the banana, the monkey would put its hand into the jar and grab onto the banana. Unwilling to let go of its food, the monkey was now stuck with a jar on its hand, which made it rather easy to catch. What does this have to do with improving the quality of your life? Everything!

When it comes to our lives, the majority of us tend to grab onto something or someone and refuse to let go. We then convince ourselves that we simply cannot survive without that person or thing and we refuse to let go. In fact, we will even hold on to people, things or habits that we consciously know are bad for us. It may be a bad relationship or job or a bad belief or physical habit. We cling to what we have—the safe, the secure and the familiar—even when we know it's unhealthy and preventing us from living a better life. And, while we want to go beyond where we are in life, most of our actions indicate that we are willing to stay exactly where and how we are. We just will not let go of our bananas, our sameness, our habits, our comfort or our past.

The monkey eventually learns that if it refuses to let go of the banana, the fruit will rot and start to stink, yet the monkey still holds on. The same is true for us. If we refuse to let go of the things or people that hold us back, life starts to rot and then stink. The only way to go beyond where you are in your life is by being willing to let go of the things, people, habits and beliefs that keep you where you are instead of where you want to be.

Letting go of your bananas begins with the power of one... one bold action, one brave decision, one limitless vision, one great question, one new idea, one burning desire or one act of kindness. As soon as you are willing to embrace the fact that you can change the quality of your life and act on that belief, your world changes for the better.

One of life's biggest challenges is the challenge of letting go. While on an educated level I am certain you can understand and appreciate what I am referring to, each of us has been created with a built-in mechanism that wants us to maintain the status quo. Despite how much we want a better life, we do tend to stick with what we know to be safe and comfortable. Face it; keeping things the same, even if your life situation is awful, is safe compared with abandoning what you have and facing the unknown. The unknown is where all of your personal and professional potential lies. The known, on the other hand, is the life you are living right now. Your choices are few and simple. Keep things as they are and resent being limited or opt for the discomfort of change as you face the unknown. As long as these choices are just about the only two choices available to you, you get to choose your destiny. Choose sameness and you get more of what you have. Choose change and letting go and a whole new world of possibilities awaits you.

Ricky Henderson, the greatest base stealer in the history of baseball, had a decision to make each time he contemplated stealing a base. He could choose not to steal the base and remain exactly where he was, or he could run the risk of leaving safety and comfort for the possibility of something greater. Ricky understood that if he wanted to get to second base, the first thing that he had to do was take his foot off first base. First base represented Ricky's banana; beyond first base lay the potential to help his team and set new standards of base stealing excellence. The same can be said of a trapeze artist. To get from one side of the net to the other, he or she must be prepared to let go. To get to a better place in your life, a place beyond your barriers, a place without rotten bananas, you must be prepared to let go of the known. Letting go of the bananas in your life requires courage and the willingness to live with the consequences of your decisions. Only those of you who are prepared to face the risks associated with letting go of the existing and embarking on the quest for a better future will have the opportunity to bask in the glow of life overflowing with personal opportunity and professional victories.

If you have chosen to remain the same, clinging onto the bananas in your life, you may as well stop reading now and gift this book to someone you know who is prepared to change his or her life. On the other hand, if you are the fearless warrior that I believe you are, this is the time when you have to decide what and who stays in your life and what and who must go. It's a tough choice. Most of your choices will involve how much you really want to bust out of your present life into a more rewarding one. The more you want to exchange your present for a more gratifying future, the more risk you will need to take. Letting go of the big bananas in your life will provide you with the opportunity for big change and big barrier busting. Or, you can play it safer and let go of the smaller bananas in your life and experience smaller change. Regardless of the choice you make, the most important thing is that you have chosen to no longer settle for your present life circumstances, and you are moving consistently and intently in the direction of your dreams.

Life is a mirror and what you see in your personal universe is an absolute mirror image of your feelings, thoughts and actions. If you perceive that you have barriers, you're right, and the only thing that really matters when you have obstacles or barriers is your level of resourcefulness. Those who want the most out of life can get it if they are highly energized and creatively resourceful. That's right; everything that exists in your present state of life is a direct reflection of all of your feelings, thoughts and actions. Change your feelings, thoughts and actions and you change your life. Change your life and your rotten bananas disappear and your barriers begin to fall. Because your life is a mirror, what you are experiencing in your life right now is also a direct reflection of all the effort and energy you have invested into the quality of your life up to this

One of life's biggest challenges is the challenge of letting go.

point in time. If you want to enjoy a better and more gratifying life—a life without bananas—you must begin by altering what you see when you look at and analyze all the aspects of your life.

All personal growth begins the moment you are willing to accept the truth about yourself. And the truth often hurts. We become so bogged down in denial that we often refuse to face or accept the truth and take personal responsibility for our lives. At one point when I was not satisfied with the condition of my life, I asked a person for whom I had tremendous admiration and respect to tell me the truth about what he thought my problem was. After making certain that I really wanted to hear it, he told me he thought I was "the most selfish person he had ever known." His comment just blew me away, and my feelings were hurt. I didn't see myself that way at all. Only after putting my ego and feelings aside was I willing to consider his comments. And when I was truly honest with myself, he was right. That one moment of truth and incredibly painful comment changed my life. You just have to face the truth about yourself if you want to tear down the barriers and let go of the stinking bananas in your life. Once you have faced and accepted the truth about who and what you *are,* as well as who and what you *are not,* you can make the decision to totally invest all of your physical and mental energy into ridding your life of all rotten bananas.

The truth for most of us is that over time it becomes increasingly easier to defend the sameness in our lives. We settle for the status quo and believe we are doomed to living the life that others have dealt us rather than taking control of our own destiny. In order to make ourselves okay with our day-to-day existence, we are capable of justifying, explaining and defending how we managed to wind up where we are. Remember, taking personal responsibility for one's life is the highest form of personal growth. In fact, I never did meet a person who couldn't perfectly explain their situation in life. Barrier busting and letting go of life's bad bananas is an ongoing tug of war between where you are and what you aspire to be. It's the constant battle between clinging to the convenience of remaining exactly where you are versus the confrontation, chaos and pain of changing the condition of your life. As I have always said, "You are in the pain or in the pain." Cling to your bananas and not like the feeling or let go of them and face the unknown. Either way you are going to be uncomfortable. My personal philosophy has always been that as long as you are going to be uncomfortable anyway, you may as well opt for the discomfort of change. Only then will you be able to fully enjoy all that life offers. Once you are willing and able to see the truth about your past you will be able to create a better present and future. Then you get to toss out all of your stale, rotten and smelly life bananas.

As I had mentioned, getting rid of your stale, rotten and smelly bananas requires courage and confidence. The reason we need so much courage is that we are literally addicted to our own lifestyles and situations. The best definition I have ever heard for an addiction is: "When you can never have enough of what you really don't want." As much as we complain and want a banana-free existence, there is a part of us that just loves our smelly, rotten and stale lifestyle. **Our approach to life is more about settling for the status quo than that of reaching for the stars.**

To advance beyond where you are you must be prepared to make some very tough decisions and willingly accept the consequences of those decisions. In life, decisions drive behavior and altered behavior creates altered outcomes. Remember, people who take emotional ownership of their lives win.

Very often, the stale bananas in your life have to do with the quality of your relationships. If your relationship bananas are working for you, that's great. On the other hand, if you are clinging to some stale, rotten and smelly relationships, you have some decisions to make. Basically, when it comes to your decision-making you have three choices…settle, fix or flee. You can keep things exactly as they are and settle for the life you have, you can fix the situation and make things better, or you can flee the situation remaining in a state of total denial. Of those choices, only you can determine what the best course of action is for your life. Just be prepared to live with the end result of those choices.

I never could understand why some people opt to remain in destructive or abusive relationships. As a child I remember members of my family who would not speak to other members of the family. Children would not talk to parents or to their siblings. When I asked my father why his brother did not speak to his father, my dad had a list of reasons that made perfect sense, at least to my uncle. While I know this isn't likely to happen in your family, these are the types of rotten bananas that can get in the way of experiencing a better life. People who choose to cling to their rotten bananas know that things are lousy, yet they just keep coming up with world-class excuses to stay where they are. Very often they are so immersed in their negative life condition that they cannot even see beyond their barriers and instead settle for a life of limitation and pain.

Improving the quality of your life takes work, focus, consistency and a burning desire to maximize the positive moments of each day of your life.

28

If that sounds like you, go get professional help now. Face it; some bananas are so big and stinky that you need help. There are people and organizations that will support you in doing what is in your own best interest. Frightening? Of course. If it were easy to let go of all of life's rotten bananas, we would live in a world that was perfect. Take a look around; life and the world are far from perfect, and that's okay, because it provides us with a challenge. Your job is to give up looking for perfection and trade it for day-to-day improvement. Remember, letting go of all of your bananas is about the daily direction that each day of your life takes. As long as you are continually moving in the right direction each day, despite how difficult that may be at times, you become closer to living a life free of limitations.

Remember, improving the quality of your life takes work, focus, consistency and a burning desire to maximize the positive moments of each day of your life. As with so many things in life there is always a trade-off. You have the ability and power to consciously choose to rid yourself of all of your personal limitations. Take stock of every single thing that holds you back and exchange those limitations for a life of limitless potential, a life that is more personally and professionally rewarding.

What You Can Do

❏ Make a list of your rotten bananas.

❏ Decide what or whom you are no longer willing to accept in your life.

❏ Be willing to get into the pain of changing your destiny.

❏ Make the tough decisions.

❏ Embrace the consequences of your decisions.

❏ Be totally honest with yourself and others.

❏ If you need help letting go of your bananas, get help.

❏ Remember, you only grow when you let go!

A person can
make it through
any "how"
if they have a
strong enough "why."

—NIETZSCHE

KEY # 2

The Dash of Life

When was your last visit to the cemetery? Yes, the cemetery. You know; the last time you visited someone's grave site. That's right, your last visit to the cemetery. In all likelihood you stood at the foot of someone's grave and read the words and dates that were etched in the granite. I have always wondered how a few words, numbers or comments etched in stone could define who a person was, what they stood for and accomplished, whose life they influenced or the content or quality of that individual's life. Well, you and I both know that there is so much more to the story than what the words in granite tell us.

As you stare at the stone, you notice the name. Is that what will define your life? Your name? Not likely, although some names do become synonymous with the accomplishments, either positive or negative, of a person's life. Good examples would be Churchill or Hitler. Both names create immediate thoughts and images in your mind. Will you be known for what you did during your life on earth? Maybe, maybe not, it's all up to you during your life and for others to judge after your life. Will the quality of your life be measured by how many years you have lived? Not necessarily; there are people that live long lives and appear to accomplish very little, while some people in a relatively short time can achieve great deeds. Will the specific date that you were born or the date that you died define your life? Probably not. The most important thing on the stone tends to be the least noticed thing on the stone…the dash. The next time you visit the cemetery to visit a loved one, just focus on the dash. In reality, it's the only thing that really matters. Let me explain.

One day a friend who I had not seen for quite a while approached me and asked, "How's your dash going?" I had absolutely no clue what he was speaking about, so when I said, "My what?" he said, "Your dash, you know, how's your dash?" Still totally lost and beginning to think more about the dashboard of my auto or about running races than living life, I asked him what he was talking about. He continued, "Your dash, your dash of life?" Enjoying my total confusion, he went on to explain that everyone is born with two dates, the date of their birth and the date of their death. Although you know the date you were born and do not know the day

> *I have always found that the people with the best Q of L—or dash of life —are those who go through life more involved in giving to others than taking from them.*

of your death, trust me, there will be the day when you no longer exist in your present form and two dates will define your time on the planet. He said that businesses, like people, also

came with two dates—the date the business began and the date
the business will cease to exist. He then explained to me that
the day of your birth or the inception of your business or the
day that you die or the death of your business is meaningless
compared to the dash that lies between the dates. He referred
to this hyphen as "the dash of life."

Though seldom noticed, when you stop to consider the
quality of your life's accomplishments, the only thing that
really matters is the dash between the dates. So while your two
dates are important, the dash between the dates signifies all of
the events of your entire life. Your dash is what truly defines
how you have lived, how you have served others and the impact you have had on the people who matter most to you and
the world in general. It's your own personal dash of life; no
two dashes are exactly the same. The dash of your life is *your*
dash and yours alone. It is a direct reflection of the choices you
have made and the decisions you have chosen to act upon.

I have always referred to the condition of an one's life as an
individual's Q of L, or Quality of Life. So, I suppose that the
question "How's your Q of L?" is just as good as asking about
someone's dash. I have always found that the people with the
best Q of L—or dash of life—are those who go through life
more involved in giving to others than taking from them. You
see, it's not what you take away from life that will ultimately
define your existence; it's what you have brought to the party
of life that makes you special to yourself and to others.

Many years ago, I took a much-needed vacation to the
island of St. Martaan. It was a vacation that I was truly excited
about, having heard so many wonderful things about the
island. On my first night I went to a highly recommended res-

taurant and ordered fish that had been caught in local waters. Unbeknownst to me some of the fish fed in areas where local industries dumped waste into the ocean, and they contained a high level of mercury. That night I became violently ill. I was unconscious for the first time in my life, had a blood pressure of 80/40—which is dangerously low—and spent 5 days in a hospital convinced that my life was over and that I would never make it off that island. As I began to slowly recover, I made some serious decisions about the rest of my life. *Live in the moment, because life is filled with the unexpected. And have fun.* From that event until now, I have lived by those rules. I plan for tomorrow but live in the now and make certain that each day is filled with joy and laughter.

In order to improve the quality of your life, your dash, there are some things you should consider doing. First, you must embark on and become involved in a program of personal improvement. Read some self-help books and act on the information; find a mentor to show you the way to a better existence and decide to be held accountable for your actions. When you do these things you are on your way to a better, more fulfilling and enjoyable existence. Taking yourself from where you are in your life to a better place begins with the decision to make you a better you!

The better you make yourself, the better you make every area of your personal and professional life and everyone with whom you come into contact. The more you elevate your standards of personal excellence, the more you will notice that the people in your sphere of influence raise their standards. Armed with the knowledge that the number one thing you can do to make your life better is to make yourself better, now is the best time to start working on you. That means that no matter the barriers that lie in the path of your personal improvement, you must be committed to doing whatever is necessary to overcome those barriers. It's not important that you like what has to be done to improve your life; you just have to do it.

I use the acronym A.U.T.O. as my guide and motivator. When confronted with a life challenge or rotten banana, I think A.U.T.O. —Around, Under, Through or Over. Any way you overcome your obstacles and blast through your barriers is okay with me. So, the next time you are faced with an obstacle, think in terms of how you can go beyond the barrier. You can go around your challenge, tunnel under the obstacle, blast through the barrier or hurdle over the problem. Regardless of how you do it, barrier busting is the way to your personal improvement. The better you make yourself, the better you make every area of your life. I strongly recommend that you utilize books, self-improvement tapes, mentors and your own personal creativity. Then dedicate each day to making yourself better.

To radically and dramatically improve your dash of life, you must approach life improvement with a "do whatever it takes" attitude. You have to totally invest yourself in your personal improvement. The more resourceful you become in making yourself better and the less willing you are to settle for the status quo, the greater your opportunity to shape your own destiny and improve the quality of your dash. As an added bonus, the better you make your own dash of life, the better you make the dash of everyone with whom you come into contact. Remember, when it comes to shedding the limitations of the past...resourcefulness rules.

The Law of Gravity is an example of an absolute Universal Law. It works every time, at least here on Earth. Because all Universal Law is absolute, it is important for you to remember that The Law of Cause and Effect has no sympathy or compassion. And, because the Law of Cause and Effect has no sympathy or compassion, it's important to remember that everything you do during the rest of your life is going to have a ripple effect. You are the Cause of your own life, and all Causes create Effects. Your present dash of life is not a coincidence. It is the end result of the situations and circumstances that occurred in your past. And, while your past dash has been predetermined and is in a place of reference, your future dash is yours to create. That means that as you prepare to move from wherever you are in your life right now to wherever you want to be, your thoughts and actions are going to have an impact. That impact may often have far reaching effects beyond your immediate world and the people in it. This is important to remember because barrier busting does come with responsibilities. And those responsibilities often go way beyond how changing your life just affects you. So, while busting your personal and professional barriers is clearly your goal as well as the purpose of this book, it's important to keep in mind that each thing you do can dramatically impact those around you. Letting go of your bananas comes with responsibilities and consequences.

I suppose what matters most at this point is the answer to the question, "How can I improve my dash of life?" Well, I have found several keys that have worked well for me and for others I have worked with who were interested in making their lives better. If you embrace these concepts, they will work for you as well…I promise. The foundation of busting all of your barriers begins with a conscious decision to make your life better. While this sounds rather simplistic, you would be amazed at how many people just live their lives each day with little or no thought about making their life better; they just survive rather than thrive. It's probably a safe bet that if you are reading this book, you want your life to improve. But beyond desiring a better life, a life free of mental and physical roadblocks, you must *believe* that you are deserving of more than you have right now. Only after you have decided to make your dash better and truly believe that you deserve a better life can you shift your focus to doing what is necessary to redefine your destiny. Remember, you cannot build a life that is better than what you believe you deserve. And, deserving a better life is a product of an improved self-image. When you feel better about yourself, you feel more deserving of better things. The more you believe you can create a better quality life, the greater the likelihood that you will attain greatness.

> *Remember, you cannot build a life that is better than what you believe you deserve.*

All change and barrier busting begins with altering your mental focus. Your mental focus is where you direct all of your mental energy at any given moment. Your ability to control your thoughts and mental energy is the key to improving the dash of your life. The sooner you can discipline yourself to consciously consider what you think about on a moment-to-moment basis, the faster the quality of your life will improve. While directing all of your mental energy into life improvement can sound and may even be overwhelming, just decide

39

to only focus on one day at a time. The more you deliberately focus on the events of each day, the more you can control the quality of your dash. Each day of your life is composed of a series of events. These events can be positive or negative, important or meaningless, and strung together they add up to another day of life. These events are spread out across the moments of each day until all 1,440 minutes have been consumed. And, at the end of each day you get to determine how wisely you have lived that day and used up your 1,440 minutes. Did you focus on making each event a positive one or not? That doesn't mean that all things that occur in a day are positive; it just means that your focus is on how you respond to what happens to you, rather than allowing those things to control you and your behavior. Of course making each day's events positive requires mental discipline, but whoever said that getting from one place to another and improving your dash of life is supposed to be simple? Facing life's challenges and overcoming roadblocks is what builds character and a person with elevated character will always do better in life.

Improving the quality of your life is a rather simple choice, and creating the mental discipline to focus on the events of each day is going to take commitment, work and dedication. At the very moment that you dedicate yourself to improving the 1,440 minutes you have to spend each day, the better your life will become. So, the beginning of improving your dash requires that you increase and improve your mental focus by thinking about what you think about. No more drifting through your day; concentrate on your thoughts the moment that you are having them. Then think about whether those thoughts are bringing you closer to or further away from a better quality of life. If your own mental feedback tells you that you are getting closer to where you want to be, you know that you are on the right track—just keep going. Improving the quality of your life should be fun. The more you make a game of focusing on your thoughts and how the quality of your thoughts can improve the quality of your dash of life, the faster you will take down all of your personal and professional barriers. Try it for just a day. There is no better day than today. That's right, today. This is not a diet and you do not have to wait until Monday to get started. You can start right now. Do it and you will be amazed at how the quality of your life starts to improve.

As you work on your minute-to-minute focus, the next thing you have to do is increase your personal energy. For 17 years of my life, I was a practicing Chiropractor in New York City. Working with thousands of patients and counseling them on everything from maintaining sound structural integrity, nutrition, exercise, proper rest and maintaining a positive attitude about their bodies and lives was both motivating and extremely fulfilling. It allowed me to witness first hand how a healthier mind and body can improve an individual's dash of life and improve an individual's physical energy. Your physical condition has a lot to do with making all of your life better. Face it, it's going to be really difficult to make your life better and go around, under, through or over your barriers if you are in rotten condition. So perhaps this the perfect time to take personal inventory and actually do something to increase your energy. While we cannot stop time from marching on, there are lots of things you can do to improve your physical condition and increase your energy. Begin with your diet and start to

41

focus on the quality of what you consume and the volume of what you consume. My personal criteria of a healthful diet are rather simple. If it looks too good and tastes too good, spit it out; it's probably bad for you. Eat in moderation and you can enjoy just about anything. In this enlightened age, you already know exactly what you have to eliminate and what you need to add to make for a healthier diet and lifestyle. And if beginning today all you did was make a few improvements in your diet, that's fine. As long as you are making changes, you are moving in the right direction, and you will begin to increase your energy level. As you start changing how and what you eat, it's important that you incorporate a program of exercise and stretching. Join a gym and actually keep going. The best way to assure you continue your workouts is to get a workout partner. You will do better and be more consistent in your exercise regime if you have someone to hold you accountable. For years my wife Laura has worked out with a personal trainer, the former Mr. Utah. As long as she has an appointment to work out and he shows up, she exercises. Without an appointment or on the days that her trainer cannot make it, no workout happens. People who want to rid their lives of smelly bananas know that being held accountable is a critical part of improving their dash of life.

So, start stretching and increasing your stamina and your body's flexibility. You will be amazed at how much more energy you will have to bust your barriers once you are eating better and exercising regularly.

Letting go of the past demands determination and if you really are intent in improving your life, you are going to have to make some bold changes and the faster you change the better. Regardless of your age or present physical condition, there are always things you can do to improve your health; and the healthier you become, the more physical and mental energy you will have. Like so many things in life, eating well and exercising regularly becomes a habit. You don't have to get radical; you just have to get started. If you do not exercise at all and do just one jumping jack a day, you begin the habit of exercise. If you eat poorly and eat just one more healthful thing a day, you are on your way to a healthier diet.

The next thing that you have to do to improve your dash is increase your level of information. The more information you can gather about improving the quality of your life, the better. Read more books, listen to personal improvement tapes and become a sponge on how to increase your happiness and health levels. For the dedicated barrier buster, a weekly visit to the bookstore is a great idea. The bookstores are loaded with great books that will guide you in developing a richer, fuller life. While you are seeking out more information, how about a visit to your local travel agency? I used to wait to take a vacation until I needed one. Well, by the time I needed one it was often too late and I was exhausted, irritable and mentally burned out. Now I

> *Make the most of each day by letting go of everything that does not figure in your future as you envision a brighter future for yourself.*

plan my vacations a year in advance. Even if those vacations are extended weekends, I always have a vacation to look forward to. If you are committed to improving your Q of L, you have to create time during which you can recharge your mental and physical batteries as well as to enjoy your family, friends and all that life has to offer.

Ultimately, improving your dash of life begins with the conscious decision to do so. You begin the moment you decide to increase your level of personal happiness. Deciding to enjoy the moments of your life and be happier is what a more fulfilling dash of life is all about. Happy people tend to be grateful for what they have and are non-judgmental of others. Being more grateful and deciding to take off your judge's robe are decisions that you can make right now. Make them. Barrier busters know that judging others damages you and the quality of your dash more than anyone else. So, give up judging and decide to be happy.

All of us eventually come to the reality that our dash can be over in a flash. The sensation that the older you get the more rapidly time passes is a real feeling. Honor that feeling and make the most of each day by letting go of everything that does not figure into the brighter future you envision for yourself.

What You Can Do

❏ Focus on each moment and work to give every minute of your life more meaning.

❏ Decide to be happy.

❏ Give up judging others.

❏ Eat right, sleep right, think right...be right.

❏ Start working on your physical condition.

❏ Visualize your barriers falling.

❏ Plan a great vacation.

❏ Believe you are worthy and deserving of a better dash of life.

*"Things turn out the best
for those who make
the best of the ways
things turn out."*

—JOHN WOODEN

KEY # 3

Increase Your Resourcefulness

Letting go of your personal and professional bananas requires that you establish a clear set of priorities about what is important to you. Only when you are crystal clear about what you really want can you create a strategy that, when followed, will take you beyond any obstacles that lie in your path. Prioritizing your desires allows you to focus your energy on the things that are most important for you to attain and moves less important priorities to the back burner.

"The things that matter most can never be at the mercy of the things that matter least." —Goethe

Until you are prepared to identify the things that matter most to you, at the expense of those things that are not quite so important, you will remain stuck with a bunch or rotten and limiting bananas. Start by making a list of what you want. Then start paring down your list until you have identified the

47

things that matter most in terms of improving the overall quality of your life. Remember, you can only think one thought at a time. The more you focus on letting go of one banana at a time, the more success you will attain.

Once you know exactly what you want, the only thing that stands in your way is how you are going to get it. This is where your level of personal resourcefulness comes in. To get from where you are right now to wherever you want to be, you must create a burning desire that fuels your every move. This internal fire has to be fueled by passion in order for you to achieve greatness in your life and blast through your personal barriers. People who are passionate about what they want will always find the personal resolve to overcome any obstacle. Passionate people are no-limit humans. They are so focused on the outcomes of their desires that they totally invest their life in the achievement of their goals. Any barrier that stands in their way is looked upon as a minor inconvenience that they have to overcome on the way to getting what they want. In short, if you want to bust your barriers and improve your life, you really have to be passionate about your desires.

Getting what you want makes it necessary for you to think beyond the obvious. The obvious has created the life you presently lead, with the bunch of bananas that you presently hold. To enjoy a better life, a life free of all barriers, you must be prepared to think beyond the obvious. The life you have right now is the end result of your thoughts, actions and emotions. In order for you to go beyond your present state, you must think, act and feel on a totally different level. You cannot improve your life by doing more of those things that created the life you presently have. Something has to change and change is your friend, even though change is going to be uncomfortable. Barrier busters understand that they cannot merely think or wish their way beyond their barriers. They recognize that, because ego and intellect are always present, those factors alone can keep people stuck behind their barriers clinging to a bunch of rotten bananas. Barrier busters accept the reality that changing their lives is going to take massive action, hard work and total dedication in order to reach whatever goals they have set for themselves.

Hard work makes dreams come true, and a great work ethic can be one of your greatest assets as you reconstruct a better future for yourself. By totally dedicating yourself to being more creative and resourceful, you will pave the way for a life that is more fulfilling as well as more fun. And because growing people create dynamic lives, make certain that you spend more time working on yourself than on anything else. When it comes to the bananas in your life, the things that stand in the way of getting what you want, the most important question is, "How much do you really want to change?" If you really

Your personal levels of resourcefulness coupled with a strong sense of urgency to make a better life for yourself are your two best friends.

want to improve your life, you will need to look within yourself and find the resourcefulness necessary to overcome your obstacles. Your personal levels of resourcefulness coupled with a strong sense of urgency to make a better life for yourself are your two best friends. People with high levels of urgency and resourcefulness can overcome any obstacle. And your urgency and resourcefulness are fueled by your personal passion. Be passionate about what you want and you will usually find a way to get it.

Resourceful people have incredibly high levels of focused energy. They do not function by the clock; rather they define their days by the accomplishment of their projects. They are willing to get up early and stay up late to change their lives. Resourceful people have incredibly high levels of physical and mental energy. They simply outperform others and, as a result, enjoy more fulfilling lives. Resourceful people are people of pure courage. They will face any challenge head on and, despite their fears, will do whatever it takes to overcome any obstacle. Becoming a person of higher energy and increasing your willingness to face any barrier head on is a matter of choice. Right now you can choose to live a better life. In this very instant you can decide to increase your levels of personal urgency and resourcefulness and make things happen in your life, instead of waiting for things to happen to you. It's a matter of choice, and when it comes to your choices, resourcefulness rules.

When our daughter Jennifer was a Brownie, she was involved in the annual Girl Scout Cookie sales competition. And as usual the competition was fierce, with each girl wanting to earn the biggest and best prize for selling the most cookies. In previous years Jennifer sold a considerable amount of cookies, but she was always outsold by one very resourceful Brownie. This year, Jennifer decided that she was going to sell the most cookies. She would not be outsold and was prepared to do whatever it took to win the competition. And so when cookie selling began, Jennifer did the usual things to sell her cookies and within a very short period of time had sold a considerable number of boxes. As the competition was coming to a conclusion, she found out that she was still behind the leader in sales—that resourceful little girl—and time was running short for turning in her orders.

Faced with the reality of possibly coming in second place again, she asked me what I thought she should do. I asked her if she really wanted to win and she said, "yes." I then asked her if she was really willing to do whatever it took to win the competition and once again she said she was. Then much to my wife's horror, I suggested that Jen take out our personal telephone directory and call one person at a time and sell them some cookies. I was amazed at Jennifer's response to the idea; she was gung ho and ready to go. She pulled up a chair, took out her order sheet and a pencil and began making phone calls to people she hardly knew. The response of the people she called was even more amazing, and within two hours Jennifer had sold an additional one hundred and fifty boxes of cookies. Feeling the tremendous pride of accomplishment, she went to bed that evening confident that she would win the competition…which she did.

> *Basically, all of life and barrier busting is like one big cookie sale. The person who wants to win the most will eventually harness the physical and mental resourcefulness to win.*

Faced with the barrier of coming in second, Jennifer had to make a choice. She could settle for less than what she wanted or she could engage her competitive spirit. She chose to apply a great sense of urgency and personal resourcefulness to what needed to be done and, fueled by the passion to win, did whatever it took to gain her victory. Basically, all of life and barrier busting is like one big cookie sale. The person who wants to win the most will eventually harness the physical and mental resourcefulness to win. Winners know that 2nd place is first loser, and when winners are determined to not settle for less than the best, they totally invest themselves in the task at hand.

When it comes to barrier busting, resourcefulness rules every time. Those with a clear vision of what they want and the personal passion to get it find the drive, energy and courage to overcome any obstacle. Their high levels of personal resolve overcome their fear of getting uncomfortable and fear of confrontation. Their burning desire and get-it-done attitude make them immune to what other people may say or think; they just get the job done.

"Things may come to those who wait, but only the things left by those who hustle." —*Lincoln*

I suppose that's it in a nutshell. The ones who hustle the most win and the ones who hustle the least watch others win. The choice is yours. You can sit on the sideline and settle for what you have or you can decide right now to overcome your personal inertia and become a "do whatever it takes" person.

"Do whatever it takes" people are always asking themselves the following question, and it's a great question for you to ask yourself as you advance in your barrier busting life: "Am I doing all that I can to win?" Keep asking yourself that question as you face any challenge and be honest with your answer. If you come up with a "yes" as your answer, you know that you are being resourceful and tip the odds in your favor of getting what you want. If you get a "no," then ask yourself, "How much do I really want it?" There are only two reasons why you do not get everything you want out of your life. You either really don't want it or you simply quit too soon. Resourceful people just don't quit!

What You Can Do

❏ Decide to no longer settle.

❏ Find your passion.

❏ Prioritize your desires.

❏ Out hustle the competition and you outdo the competition.

❏ Each day, ask yourself, "Am I doing all that I can to win"?

❏ Never give in and never give up.

KEY # 4

Finding Your Bananas

Fact...we all have bananas, things that hold us back. If you cannot see yours, you are just not trying. Denying that you have obstacles that stand in the way of making a better life for yourself and your loved ones will not make your life situation better. In fact, refusing to admit to yourself that you are stuck can seriously diminish your dash of life. If you are uncertain about what your barriers are, just ask someone you love and trust to point them out to you. Be prepared to not necessarily like or agree with what you hear. Facing up to the reality of who you are can often be painful as well as eye opening. Yes, the truth can hurt and getting into the pain of reality is healthy even though it's uncomfortable. It has been said that the true measure of a person is often determined by how much truth they can take without having their feelings hurt. Face it, you have roadblocks and obstacles that are getting in the way of you living the life you desire most. And, until you are ready, willing and able to accept the fact that you probably have an entire bunch of bananas to let go of, very little change and improvement can or will occur in your life.

Bananas come in all shapes and sizes. In fact, some of your bananas are actually shaped like people. Some bananas are real while others are perceptions and exist only in your imagination. Whether real or perceived, a barrier is a barrier, and those barriers stand in your way of a better future. If you carefully examine the things that are holding you back, I believe you will find that most of your barriers have been created in two different ways. You either created them on your own to remain safe and comfortable or you intentionally or unintentionally bought into another person's viewpoint of you and your potential. Regardless of whether your barriers are big or small, real or vividly imagined, self-created or dumped on you by another person, you get to decide whether you want to tolerate them or go beyond them. Tolerating them and leaving your barriers exactly as they are means that you have chosen to remain in sameness. Selecting to go beyond your present place indicates that you are working in the direction of creating a better life for yourself. All success in life begins with a decision. And, by deciding that you are prepared to do whatever it takes to go around, under, through or over your barriers is the beginning point of a better and brighter future.

Bananas basically come in five varieties: physical bananas, mental bananas, emotional bananas, economic bananas and social bananas. Regardless of the kinds of barriers that you cling to, the important thing to remember is that when it comes to letting go of the things that hold you back, resourcefulness rules. People that possess a high level of resourcefulness will eventually thrive in their lives rather than remain stuck and merely exist. Resourcefulness is the essential ingredient in letting go of limitations and designing a life without roadblocks. The more you want a better life and the more you adopt the habits of the people with fulfilling lives, the more likely you are to have a better life—if you are willing to get into the pain of change and personal growth.

I lived in the beautiful ski town of Park City, Utah. Whenever possible I would take advantage of the incredible snow conditions and hit the slopes for a day of skiing. Hardly a day passed on the mountain when I did not see special limitless people doing extraordinary things. Skiers paralyzed from the waist down skiing in special seats. Amputees, some with only one leg or arm, doing things others think about doing but find reasons not to. Sightless people skiing with the assistance of sighted ski guides. These brave, resourceful and remarkable people had some choices. They could choose to live limited lives—and have the perfect excuses for not excelling—or accept the hand they were dealt and choose to enjoy all that life offers, despite physical challenges that would hold others back. Each of us has some sort of physical challenge; so what? Perhaps it's the challenge of our height or weight; so what? Maybe we are not as attractive as some other people; so what? We may be handicapped in some way or perhaps it's just the years having taken their toll; so what? These are all great excuses to not do something with our lives,

> *Do whatever it takes to win and always remember that in order to live a more successful life, you have to give more than you take away.*

and every excuse I have ever heard always made perfect sense to the person with the excuse. But resourcefulness rules, and if you are truly determined to win, in spite of real or perceived physical limitations, you will.

Mentally, I suppose we are all limited, if we choose to see ourselves that way. There is always a person with a higher IQ, if that's what you want to use as a yardstick for measuring a person's potential. However, the world is filled with incredibly bright people who cannot seem to get out of their own way. Other individuals who some would consider less intelligent manage to create greatness in their lives. The bottom line: they just want to succeed more. They refuse to accept the labels placed on them by others, and through sheer willpower, a powerful work ethic and dedication, they create the habit of an achiever. So what if you are not the sharpest tool in the shed? Resourcefulness Rules. Just decide right now to make up for shortcomings with other skills. Do whatever it takes to win and always remember that, in order to live a more successful life, you have to give more than you take away. It's the opposite of eating celery. When you eat celery you lose more calories in eating than you gain in calories. I suppose if a person ate only celery, he would eventually disappear. Just make certain that you bring more to the game of life than you take away, and your rotten bananas will fall by the wayside.

It has taken me years of studying people to figure out, but I finally have come to the conclusion that all of us are screwed up. Some more than others and some more visibly than others but basically each of us have moments when we are a little bit crazy. We all have some emotional hang-ups and barriers that keep us where we are and prevent us from moving forward.

Regardless of our background and despite how much our loved ones tried to create a perfect child, we each have some emotional blocks that prevent us from advancing to a better place in our lives. Me? I've got a bunch of them. In fact I may hold the personal record for emotional bananas. The most glaring is probably my lack of tolerance. I work on being more tolerant of others and life situations on a daily basis, and I have come to realize that my intolerance has gotten in the way of better relationships and a happier existence. So, each day I wake up knowing that to fully enjoy the day and the people I will encounter, I have to be more accepting of others and simply cannot have everything perfect or the way that I want it to be. Whatever your emotional barrier is—*if* there is one—to improve your life you must work diligently on coming to the truth about who you are, accepting who you are and consciously striving to make each day better.

If an economic or financial barrier is holding you back, it probably has to do with the lack of money. After all, very few people that I know have too much money! The rotten banana of not enough money can destroy marriages, businesses and put tremendous stress on one's life. I believe that having more money is a mindset. There is an abundance of money in the Universe; you just have to be willing to do whatever it takes to earn it, legally of course. I have never seen a daily newspaper without a "help wanted" section. In a world where people will have more then one career in their lifetime, perhaps it's time to explore what lies beyond what you are presently doing. Change, although scary for some, is your friend when it comes to improving your financial state. There are always people looking for people to work for money. Overcoming your economic barriers begin with the belief that you are deserving of more and concludes with you increasing your determination and work ethic. Once again, resourcefulness rules and the person who wants it the most always figures out a way to thrive.

Social barriers usually have to do with how you feel about yourself. Those who have a difficult time in social situations traditionally have feelings of low self-esteem. They just do not feel confident with others and go out of their way to avoid situations that make them uncomfortable. Obviously, if you want to advance in life you have to be willing to place yourself in situations that further your advancement. So, the more comfortable you become in social situations, the more you increase your opportunities to overcome your life barriers.

How do you get more confident and improve your level of self-esteem? Simple, you dedicate yourself to doing so and work on your confidence level on a daily basis. A good place to start is with your eye contact. Low self-esteem people usually have a difficult time establishing and holding eye contact with anyone they feel intimidated by. So decide to get uncomfortable and start looking into the eyes of

Finding your area of personal greatness and maximizing your talents is the key to busting your barriers.

whoever you are speaking with and maintain eye contact until the conversation is over. Sure it's uncomfortable, that's the idea…to get intentionally uncomfortable until we overcome our obstacle. Discomfort is good; it's how we grow as people, and the more you are willing to get uncomfortable, the greater your human potential. It's also a good idea to hit the bookstore shelves. The self-improvement section is full of books on how you can improve your self-esteem and the condition of your life. The better you think about yourself, the more barriers you will bust. Remember, you can only create a life up to your level of self-worth. The more you like you, the more your life improves.

Your mission, once you have identified your personal barriers, is to dedicate yourself to overcoming them on a daily basis. The more you change yourself, the more you change your life. Make yourself the very best person you can be, and you start losing the negative and limiting bananas of your past. And the more you let go of the past, the more you enjoy your future. In life you get what you deserve. You earn the right to deserve more when you increase your personal self-worth.

Remember, it's okay to have bananas/barriers; it's just not okay to use them as the excuses that explain the condition of your life.

As you make yourself better and begin to move beyond your barriers, you will literally shed negative mental energy as you go. Shedding negative energy and becoming a more positive and uplifting person requires a tremendous amount of personal discipline. You must be extremely aware of your thoughts, because negative mental thoughts can and will diminish your personal power. To shed negative energy, imagine that each day you have to take out your mental garbage. Visualize a large garbage can and each time you have a limiting or negative thought you take that thought and put it in the can. Then, at the end of each day, take out your garbage. The object of this exercise is to keep you conscious about your thoughts and eventually have days with only positive, uplifting and limitless thoughts and emotions. Imagine an empty garbage can at the end of each day and how much better your life would be without negativity and limitation.

I believe that every person comes equipped with the innate ability to excel in at least one area of life. Finding your area of personal greatness and maximizing your talents is the key to busting your barriers. Unleashing your natural gifts requires that you get in touch with those things in life that you are passionate about. People who are passionate about improving their lives and the lives of others win. For only after you have discovered your true gift as a person can you create a life strategy that will allow you to overcome all of your barriers.

Is identifying and working to overcome your barriers easy? That's a judgment you will ultimately get to make. Change can be as easy or as difficult as you make it. And if letting go of the known in exchange for the unknown frightens you, that's okay. Will you have setbacks along the way? Possibly, and if you do, that's okay as well. Letting go of the things in your life is about your personal tenacity and your desire to persevere regardless of the challenge. At the very moment that you decide to only accept a world without the people, situations and circumstances that hold you back, you can alter your destiny.

What You Can Do

❏ Acknowledge that you have some bananas/barriers.

❏ Be honest and identify what your barriers are.

❏ Stop judging yourself.

❏ Do whatever it takes to make you better each day.

❏ Find your personal passion.

❏ Do what you love and love what you do.

❏ Work to increase your level of personal resourcefulness.

"Let no feeling of discouragement prey upon you, and in the end you are sure to succeed."

—ABRAHAM LINCOLN

KEY # 5

Win the Blame Game

When it comes to letting go of your bananas, there is no substitute for taking responsibility for your own life. Regardless of who or what created your present set of circumstances, from this moment on you get to determine your own destiny. And, while accepting that fact is liberating, the feeling and knowledge that you are now responsible for your future can be both exciting and frightening. On the one hand you have the ultimate freedom to imagine any future you desire, and on the other hand you realize that the instant you take responsibility for your life, the blame game must come to an end. It's all up to you.

The blame game is our way of assigning the condition of our lives to outside forces. When an aspect of our lives doesn't live up to our expectations or the expectations of others, we look for other people or life situations that will perfectly explain why we are how we are. Rather than take responsibility for our own life, it's just easier and a lot less painful to find someone or something else to blame for what we haven't yet accomplished in our lives than to take total and complete responsibility. The blame game is an ego defense mechanism that we employ to keep us feeling good about ourselves, as we perfectly justify and defend our present place in life. The blame game has nothing to do with our life accomplishments; rather the blame game is played to explain the areas where we have fallen short of our expectations.

At one time or another, each of us has blamed others for the condition of our lives, and it always seems to make perfect sense to us. It doesn't make a difference how you got your bunch of bananas or who gave them to you. Always remember that most people proceed through life with an agenda. So how you got to this place in your life may have to do with the influence of others; regardless of how you got your rotten bananas, it's your bunch and it's time that you took responsibility for them. With the exception of the people who take responsibility for their lives, every person that I have met who didn't have a perfect life did have a perfect explanation as to why his or her life wasn't perfect; it's their story. Defending the status quo and past is always easy to do; building a better future requires determination, dedication and courage. If you are committed to busting your personal and professional barriers, the blame game must come to an end right now. It's time to face reality, and reality for most of us is that our parents, teachers and preachers did the very best they could. Nobody has the perfect childhood or life and each of us has been saddled with different physical, mental and emotional challenges to overcome if we want to achieve greatness in our lives.

It has been said that the reason the windshield of an automobile is larger than the rear view mirror is because you are supposed to spend more time looking where you are going than where you have been. Life is like that too. To live a successful life, look where you are going and stop focusing on where you've been. Stop defending and explaining and accept the past for exactly what it is—the past. If you want to bust all of your barriers and enjoy banana-free living, you must accept the responsibility and reality that you have a lot more influence over tomorrow than you do over yesterday. Look forward and recognize that wherever you are right now is the place you need to grow from. No more blame game, just accepting total and complete responsibility for the rest of life's journey. Your past is supposed to be a place of reference, not a place of residence. You can learn from the past, you just don't have to live there. The more you choose to reside in and dwell on your past, the more difficult it will be for you to create a better future for yourself. You can refer to your past and you can learn from past occurrences, but you are not supposed to live in your past. Accept your past for exactly what it is, the thing that brought you to where you are today. Nothing more and nothing less. Your past was predestined, but your future is yours to create and you improve it by taking responsibility for what happens next in your life.

Successful living is all about what you decide

> *The easiest way to eliminate the blame game from your life is to live in the present, plan for the future and accept the past.*

to do next. Not what you plan on doing, not what you think about doing, but what you actually will do next. "Next" is a powerful word especially when you want to get from one part of your life to another. Focusing your energy on what needs to be done next will allow you to continue moving forward with your life, while putting little or no energy into what has occurred in your past. Your "next" is your future and that's where you should put your mental energy. After all, you are going to spend the rest of your life in your future, not in your past. And, the more you decide to enjoy your "now" as you plan your "next," the more fun and fulfillment you will have in your life. As an added bonus, the more you live in the "now" and focus on what happens "next" in your life, the less the emotion of guilt will play in your life.

The easiest way to eliminate the blame game from your life is to live in the present, plan for the future and accept the past. When you live in the moment, you get more value and enjoyment out of life. When you plan for your future, you always have something wonderful and exciting to look forward to. When you accept your past, you begin to take responsibility for your life. Sounds healthy to me!

When we look at our lives, especially if we are not happy with what we see, our natural tendency is to look outside of ourselves for the solution. Well, the answer to making your life better does not reside on the outside; the solutions to our lives is an inside job. Instead of looking for solutions, as of this moment you can decide to be your own solution. At a particularly difficult time for me in business, when things weren't going as I thought they should, I spent considerable time and money looking into my past and trying to find out why I was stuck. With little success and still frustrated, a friend suggested that I put my energy into a better place. What he said changed my life. He said, "Forget how you got to where you are, just focus on what you need to do next." That was such an eye opener for me, and from that moment on my life has been more gratifying. Stop looking for solutions; be your own solution. Now that's what I call taking total and complete responsibility for your life.

Conquering blame and taking responsibility also requires that you give up all of your negative feelings toward yourself and others. Letting go of your negative bunch of bananas is a healthy decision, because as long as you remain anchored to your negative emotions about yourself or others, you will be prevented from attaining your personal greatness. Negative emotions can literally own you and virtually all of your negative emotions are feelings about past events or people. It's impossible to build a better future if your emotions are rooted in the past. Excuse and accept yourself and others for what and who they are, hang up your judge's robe and wipe the slate clean of past negative events. The moment that you do, you pave the way for a better tomorrow. So, let go and get going.

Working to eliminate your fears, worries and anxieties also demands great personal resolve. To tear down all of your barriers and rid yourself of your rotten bananas, you really have to be committed to changing your behaviors and making a better life for yourself. And, letting go of your anger toward others is an important step in creating a healthier, happier you. When you are angry, whatever or whomever you are angry with takes control of your emotions and literally takes charge of your behavior. You are powerless when you are angry because anger toward others causes you to surrender control of your life; and when you are out of control of your life, it is impossible to create a better future for yourself. It's also time to give up your fears and anxieties. Your fears, worries and anxieties stifle your imagination and, when your imagination is inhibited, you limit your personal potential. I know that giving up your fears is a lot easier to talk about than it may be to do, and that's usually true. Just keep in mind that conquering the tough stuff in your life is what shapes your character and alters your opportunities for a better future. Barrier busting demands courage. The best way to display your courage is to turn your fears, worries and anxieties into the stepping-stones for attaining your personal greatness. Most of your fears and anxieties were created by real or imagined life events and previous life experiences. And, while your fears and anxieties are real, even if they are illogical, you already know that most of the things that you fear are more frightening in your mind than they ever could be in your reality. Most of our fears and anxieties are created by our feeling of lack of control over a situation or thing. The moment you accept the reality that you cannot control every aspect of your life, and that eventually you have to begin to trust others, you are well on your way to busting your barriers.

Conquering the tough stuff in your life is what shapes your character and alters your opportunities for a better future.

Overcoming your fears and anxieties requires trust, and when you willingly give up the need to control situations and decide to increase your trust in yourself and others, your fears will begin to melt away. Remember, if you are looking for reasons to stay exactly the way you are, there are usually great reasons all around you. However, if you want to get past the reasons in your life and enjoy better results in your life, the time to let go of the past is now. And, while letting go of the past isn't always easy, letting go of the negative emotions of your past and ridding yourself of your fears, worries and anxieties is always worthwhile.

I received my driver's license at age seventeen. And, like most new drivers, the more time I could spend behind the wheel, the better. I loved to drive. Driving was cool, driving was the grown up thing to do and a great way to impress the other kids who weren't driving yet. One day, with no particular place to go, I loaded a bunch of friends into the car and went for an innocent joy ride in upstate New York. As I rounded a bend in the road, I noticed a young boy riding his bicycle on the shoulder of the country road. Just as I was overtaking him, he turned his bike into the side of my car. Everything happened so fast. The terrible crash, the sudden impact, the crumpled bicycle and the blood of the boy's head on my shattered windshield. To say this was a horrible tragedy is an understatement. My life changed in an instant, as did that of everyone else in the car. The police arrived, the ambulance came, and we were all escorted to the nearest emergency room. The last thing I ever wanted to do again at that moment was drive, and the first thing the officers insisted that I do was get behind the wheel and resume driving. At the emergency room the minutes seemed like hours. Eventually the doctor appeared to inform us that the boy had died of head wounds from the accident. We were all beside ourselves with grief. That unfortunate accident left a family without a son and all of us with a real dose of how fragile life can be. To this day, the events of that one afternoon remain with me every time that I pass a person on a bicycle. But I pass the bicycle rider in spite of my experience of the past and the anxiety of what might happen. Successful living requires that you continually move forward in spite of the past.

In order for you to let go of your bananas and overcome your personal obstacles, you have to improve the quality of your choices in life. You can either remain stuck, blaming your past for limiting your future, or you can make the tough decision to accept total and complete responsibility for the rest of your life. By giving up the blame game and going positively forward regardless of your past, you have actively taken responsibility for your future. A successful life is nothing more than a series of successful choices. The more you focus on the quality of your thoughts, the better life becomes for you. The choice is yours to make. Choose wisely.

What You Can Do

❑ Totally accept who you are.

❑ Forgive anyone that you hold a grudge against.

❑ Take responsibility for your life choices from this day forth.

❑ Live in the present, plan for the future and accept the past.

❑ Give up your fears, worries and anxieties... it's a choice.

❑ Focus only on what is about to happen "next."

"If everything seems under control, you're just not going fast enough."

—Mario Andretti

KEY # 6

Your Bananas Are In Your Head

The bottleneck is always at the top of the bottle! And, most of our barriers/bananas/limitations exist in our heads long before they ever live in our reality. Your brain is where your mind lives and letting go of your limitations is a matter of mind set. In order for you to change your life, you must be prepared to change your mind. Only when you are willing to think beyond your present life situation can you dramatically improve the quality of the rest of your life.

You have all heard the expression, "A mind is a terrible thing to waste." Well, it's true. Most of us go through life without even coming close to using our mental capacity to the maximum. The more you engage your mind and use it like a tool to improve your life and bust your barriers, the more fulfilling your life will be.

I wish I could remember where I picked up the following slice of wisdom because I believe that it speaks to the very heart of just how important it is to take charge of the environment in which our minds dwell:

Leaders are like eagles. They don't flock; you find them one at a time.
Control your Thoughts…for they will become your Words.
Control you Words…for they will become Actions.
Control your Actions…for they will become your Habits.
Control your Habits…for they will become your Character.
Control you Character…for it will become your Destiny.

Letting go of your bananas is a head space, an attitude and a decision to no longer accept the situations, people and things that hold you back. And the big shift from where you are to where you want to be starts with the quality of your thoughts. Everything else that you will create in your life will flow directly from the way you think. If you want a different life experience, you must be willing to think on another level. Your previous thoughts account for the behaviors that have created the life you have right now. Change your thoughts going forward and those new thoughts will create new behaviors, behaviors that will alter your life and free you of personal and professional limitations.

All barrier busting is about your desire to move forward, in spite of the limitations of the past. Barrier busting is all about direction. To free yourself of a past filled with rotten bananas, all of your mental energy has to be centered on moving forward rather than being anchored in old thoughts and behaviors. For you to advance beyond your present place, regardless of how long you have been stuck in that place, you must think, act and vividly imagine yourself on the other side of where you currently are. When you think, act and imagine yourself beyond your present place, your life will begin to move forward in a positive and constructive way. Now is the time to fully engage the power of your mind and utilize that power to create a better future for yourself.

When you engage your imagination and vividly envision where you want to be, you have taken the first step in realizing all of your dreams. So, to change where and how you are in life, you must change what you see in your mind's eye. The subconscious mind is the part of your mind that works like a robot. That means that your subconscious mind works for you and is powered by repetition, your imagination and your decisions. Even better, your subconscious mind always accepts your desires as attainable and always responds with a "yes" when you desire something. It does not question, it just delivers what you want. Whatever you imbed in your subconscious mind is accepted as truth, and whatever you accept as your truth can ultimately become your reality. That's right; you can use the power of your mind to think your way to greatness, to rid yourself of life's barriers and to alter your destiny. All you have to do is get a crystal clear image of what you want in your life and where you want to be. Once you lock onto your desires, almost as if by magic you can attract into your life all of the opportunities that will allow you to get what you want. Now that's powerful! Change your mind and you change your life. Change your mind and you reshape your destiny.

The key to banana-free living is to only define yourself based on how you are going to be when you are free of all of your bananas. All of your physical and mental energy has to be totally invested in the image of the new banana-free you. Decide right now to only see yourself as the person who no longer holds on to a limiting past, and you are free. No longer do you have the luxury of wallowing in your past or using your past as the excuse for where you are right now. All of your focus, all of your energy, all of your actions, all of your words, all of your decisions and all of your mental images must focus on how you are going to be when you are the ultimate you. Becoming the best you can be begins with a decision fostered by a strong visual image. That image is what will engage you in action, with each action designed to bring you closer to the ultimate you. Bottom line…the sum total of all of your thoughts and all of your actions will alter your outcomes in life.

To create a better life, you must use the power of your mind to mentally step outside of your current beliefs.

I am not talking about merely wishing yourself to a better life. "If wishes were horses, beggars would ride," as the expression goes. Wishing is nice, but just wishing is not the ingredient that barrier busters use to improve their lives. Those who let go of their limiting bananas understand that whatever they want to achieve in life must be accompanied by a commitment to a program of personal growth and driven by strong determination. By always mentally moving toward what you want, you put separation between you and your limited past. To go beyond your present place, you must think beyond your present thoughts. That means you have to actually think about your thoughts on a moment-to-moment basis. In truth, most of us go through our lives with little regard for the importance of our thoughts. We run based on habit and spend very little time examining how each thought and action impacts our lives. We are just happy to make it from one day to the next with as little inconvenience as possible. So, we cruise through life and settle rather than consciously work toward making each day as good as it can be. We are inclined to believe that the life we have is probably as good as our life can be and that thought becomes our belief.

Your past belief about the quality of the rest of your life has created the life you presently have. To create a better life, you must use the power of your mind to mentally step outside of your current beliefs. Only by letting go of your current beliefs can you create a new set of beliefs that support a better future for yourself. Seeing yourself as an individual who is free of the barriers of the past is empowering and liberating.

People who are empowered to think limitless thoughts and envision a life of extraordinary freedom enjoy massive doses of personal serenity. Your personal serenity is a key element in the quality of your life. Happy and serene people are fun to be with and stand as a positive influence and role model for others. Serenity is a choice that each of us can make when we are free of our rotten bananas. Attaining your personal serenity demands that you acknowledge the successes you have already enjoyed in life and give yourself credit for your achievements. When you mentally reward yourself for past achievements, you build your confidence and self-image. Feeling better about yourself will pave the way for greater accomplishments as you rid yourself of your limitations and create a more dynamic and confident you. Remember, your thoughts and mental images are the seeds of your personal and professional greatness. Your greatness is defined by your imagination; and the more you are willing to embrace and visualize a better life for yourself, the more you will be free of the past and all of its limitations. When you engage your imagination to envision a better life for yourself, you are viewing your life beyond the obvious. The obvious is the life that you are living at present. Beyond the obvious are all of the opportunities that you will need to bust all of your barriers and rid yourself of the rotten bananas of your past.

When it comes to fulfilling your personal potential, the more time you invest in planning your future, the better your future will be. There are no coincidences in life—you pretty much get what you expect and strive for. You can either exist from day to day and just let life happen to you, or you can direct your mental energy to seeing how your life will be when you attain all of your desires. Your creative mind provides you with a limitless mechanism to conceive a better life for yourself. Set high goals for yourself and you move closer to a better life for yourself. Daring to think beyond what's reasonable and venturing into outrageous thoughts will create new and exciting opportunities for you. Thinking outrageously requires that you stop being logical and start being limitless in your thoughts and plans.

Make all of your plans and decisions with the greater good in mind. When you choose to change your life for the greater good, what's in the best interest of yourself and others, your life takes on greater meaning and the achievements of your life become more worthwhile. As you strive to achieve the greater good in your life, realize that the logical mind will seldom alter an emotion or feeling. The only ways to alter emotions are with other emotions, and the more emotionally excited and passionate you are about your limitless potential, the further you will go toward your dreams. If you can think it and see it in your mind's eye, you can have it, as long as you are willing to pay the price of attainment.

Remember, there is a very big difference between motivation and willpower. Motivation tends to come from an outside source and is very often short in duration. I have never seen a person who relied on motivation accomplish long-term success in their lives. However, the people who I know that have the internal drive created by sheer willpower seem to be able to work miracles. They function with great clarity about their goals, certainty about achieving their goals, and they continually move in the direction of their desires. Willpower comes from passion, and when you are passionate about something you will be inspired to greatness.

Because all of your bananas are in your head, the more you constructively control your thoughts the better the odds of reaching your greatest potential. When you take control of your thoughts and mental images you can literally transform your life. Not just alter your life, but also transform your life. The mind works in pictures, not in words. Your words do create images in your mind, and when you lock onto those images what you envision can become your reality. When you engage and direct your vivid imagination toward what you want, you can change your world. The power of the mind is awesome; use it to your advantage!

What You Can Do

❏ **Only think about yourself in terms of how you are going to be when you become the ideal you.**

❏ **Control what you think about and you control your destiny.**

❏ **Think outrageous thoughts to create outrageous results.**

❏ **Always strive to create the greater good in all that you do.**

❏ **Maintain a consistently open mind.**

❏ **Work on your personal serenity.**

*The greater the adversity,
the greater your personal
potential.*

The 3 Essentials to Banana-Free Living

L ike so many of you, a great deal of my life has been filled with stress, strife and struggle. And, while many will argue that these ingredients are the building blocks of personal character, I believe that there are a lot of ways to build your character without having to suffer and be miserable.

In my life I have been blessed with people who have taken an interest in helping me achieve my personal potential. These people took the time to share with me their formulas for personal and professional success, and by employing their methods I have dramatically changed my life as I let go of the rotten bananas of my youth. Basically, I have culled their teachings down to what I consider to be the three essentials for creating a life that is free from all bananas. You have to believe that you deserve a life without limits, obstacles, barriers or anchors that connect you to your past experiences. Remember, your past exists for you to learn from, not for you to replicate for the rest of your life.

The three essentials that I learned are:
1. maintain a willingness to be coached,
2. develop a consistently powerful work ethic, and
3. always be crystal clear about the direction of your life.

Very few people have the capacity to dramatically and permanently change their lives by themselves. If you are willing to admit that you need some help and support in transforming your life, the next thing you need to do is find a transformation coach. Coaches come in many forms and in many instances you may require more than one coach to help you free yourself of your barriers. Coaches exist in every area of life, and once you know exactly what you want, you can and will find someone who will be willing to support you in achieving your personal and professional aspirations. I believe that we tend to cling to comfort. Comfort in life is not bad unless it prevents us from moving forward and we become bogged down in a rut. Human nature causes us to go with what we know, both in situations and relationships. It's that thirst for safety, security and sameness that very often causes us to settle into a life that is habitual rather than challenging and stimulating. When that happens our tendency is to stop striving for greatness. That's where your transformational coach comes in.

A coach is very different than a teacher. A teacher will tell you or show you what to do. The purpose of a coach is to tell you what to do, show you how to do it and hold you personally accountable for the completion of your tasks. A great coach will take on the responsibility of holding you accountable. Without a high level of personal accountability, very little permanent change takes place. Of course, having a coach and being "coachable" are two distinctly different things. Being coachable literally means that you are licensing another person to hold you accountable to doing whatever is necessary in order for you to achieve your personal greatness.

Coaching and accountability are the two major ingredients of all championship sports franchises. The coach assumes the responsibility to hold the player accountable and the player that is committed to winning does what the coach says even if he or she doesn't like it. A great coach is a mentor who creates a system that keeps you moving in

Maintain a willingness to be coached.

the direction of what you have mutually agreed to accomplish. Both the coach and the person being coached must be in total agreement about the desired outcome of their efforts. It is the responsibility of a coach to bring out the very best in his or her performers. This can often be done by continually reminding you of what is possible to achieve when you are inspired by a passionate vision. Remember, what others have done, you can do. And what already has been done can be surpassed by the totally committed performer who is willing to let go of their beliefs and exchange them for a grander vision.

Developing a great work ethic is a product of desire, determination and decisiveness. Very often our work ethic is created by what we observe during the formative years of our lives. And while most people believe they work hard, the ultimate determining factor about our work habits can be measured by our outcomes. Work ethic should be evaluated by much more than the amount of hours we spend at what we are doing. Work ethic must be judged by the outcomes we create with the time, effort and energy we invest in improving the quality of our lives and the lives of those around us. The critical factor in evaluating our work ethic has to do with realistic self-evaluation. At the end of each day ask yourself the following question: "Did my efforts today bring me closer to what I really want, and within the time frame that I have set for myself?" If you can honestly answer "yes" to that rhetorical question, then you know for certain that your work ethic is consistent with the kind of changes that you want in your life.

Remember, all change is about direction and as long as you continually move in the direction of what you

Develop a consistently powerful work ethic.

want, eventually you will shed the bananas that hold you back and realize your true personal potential.

Barrier busting behavior begins in the mind with a conscious decision and then must manifest itself in every aspect of your daily routine. Hard work and smart work make dreams come true.

When it comes to improving the quality of your life and letting go of your limiting bananas, there simply is no substitute for clarity. I believe that **a clear vision is the genius of all creation.** At the very moment you know exactly what you want in your life and exactly what you are no longer willing to accept in your life, you grow closer to the goals that you have set for yourself. Clarity is about what we see for ourselves in our mind's eye. The majority of what we have learned in our lives has been learned visually. We are visual beings and the more we visualize exactly what our life is going to be like in the future, the more the powers of our subconscious mind will begin to bring us closer to the opportunities that will alter our destiny.

Once you are clear about what you want and what it looks like, put your desires in writing. To know what you want is never quite enough if you want to let go of the past and shape a brighter future. Your desires must be committed to paper. Simply put, it it's not in writing, it doesn't exist. And to enhance the written word, add visual images. The clearer you are about what you want, the easier it becomes to recognize opportunities when they appear. In order to make certain that your thoughts and actions are only about what you want and not about what you presently have, you must develop the discipline of "thinking about what you are thinking about." That means that your level of consciousness about your self-talk and thoughts needs to be carefully monitored. And, any time you entertain thoughts that limit your potential, you must refocus your mental energy and bring yourself back to the life you envision for yourself. This one action alone will have a profound impact on every moment of your existence. As soon as you master the skill of closely monitoring your thoughts, you will notice how much more enjoyable your days are. When you know exactly where you are going, the road to your destination will become apparent.

A banana-free existence awaits the person with great clarity of vision, an extraordinary work ethic and a coaching system that is steeped in accountability.

What You Can Do

❏ Find an accountability coach.

❏ Decide to be held to a higher standard of excellence.

❏ Model the barrier-busting habits of others who have let go of their limitations.

❏ Take control of your thought process.

❏ Improve your work ethic.

❏ Create a clear vision about your future.

❏ Live in the now.

KEY #8

Fearlessness

L iving a life free of rotten bananas requires that you identify and face your fears and then overcome them. And, while most would agree that the vast majority of the things we fear rarely occur, we can often be paralyzed by the very thought of what might happen to us if we dare to move beyond our present level of self-imposed comfort. Keep in mind that the acronym for FEAR is False Evidence Appearing Real. When you begin to accept that most of the things we fear are self-induced, you can work to better control your thoughts.

Face it; fear is one of our most powerful emotions and one of our greatest motivators. It can consume our thoughts, destroy relationships, limit us in business and prevent us from living a life without limitations. For the majority of us, our emotions play a significant part in our decision-making. We tend to weigh the balances of our decisions, consider the consequences of our behaviors and evaluate what may happen to us if we change the way we live our lives. All of this mental energy creates real feelings and those real feelings very often influence our decisions and lives. The challenge to living a life free of fearful bananas ultimately has to do with understanding our emotions. Sometimes in the face of extraordinary logic we are still bogged down by the things that we fear most.

Remember, if you are highly emotional about your fear, all of the logic in the world is not going to change how you feel. So, if that's the case, how do we let go of our fears and create a limitless, more productive life?

Simple, you use a more powerful emotion than the emotion of fear to change your destiny. So while all of the logic in the world can still leave you stuck, a more powerful emotion can drive personal and professional change. For example, what if you are afraid of public speaking and have difficulty standing up and making a presentation in front of an audience? Public speaking has always been regarded as one of the most common fears that plagues people. We place such tremendous importance on the need to be liked; running the risk of rejection by presenting in front of others can paralyze us.

A friend of mine has that exact fear. Already a very successful businessman, he understands that his business growth has been diminished because of this fear. He is a dynamic, persuasive and powerful communicator one-on-one, but with a couple of other people in the room he froze. It didn't matter if he knew the people or not. When it came to a public address, regardless of how short the address was, he just couldn't overcome the fear. ***Passion eats fear for lunch.*** One day during a business meeting we were discussing his fear and we began to calculate exactly how much business/dollars he was losing as a result of his fear of public speaking. The numbers were staggering…one very big smelly, rotten and limiting banana was standing in the way of allowing his business to skyrocket.

So, right then and there, faced with the reality of what he was losing vs. what he could be gaining in business, a far more powerful emotion kicked in…the emotion of passion. In this instance, the realization of what he could be creating for himself, his family and employees elicited a powerful desire to succeed in business beyond his current success.

In business and in life, in order to alter your destiny, you must always be prepared to sacrifice the thing, people or situations that hold you back in exchange for the things that matter most. At the very moment that you face your fears and decide to find a greater residual benefit to enhance your life, you change. When you become crystal clear about improving your life and identify what you need to give up in order for you to arrive at a happier, healthier and more successful place, you will begin the process of giving up your fears and limiting bananas.

Identify your fears and understand that the things you fear most very often stop you from having the things that you want most. With time, honesty and courage, you can come to recognize

> *In business and in life, in order to alter your destiny, you must always be prepared to sacrifice the thing, people or situations that hold you back in exchange for the things that matter most.*

and understand your fears. Then, you can begin to manage the emotions that your fears create and recognize exactly what your fear is costing you in terms of the quality of your life. Once you do that, you can search for a passionate reason or a more powerful emotion, to go beyond your present place in life.

Bottom line…it's okay to be afraid. In fact, there are probably plenty of times or situations in our past that, at the time, scared us to death. And yet when we look back at most of those situations, our fears of the past seem over dramatized and we wonder what we were so afraid of in the first place.

Remember, a little fear is not a bad thing. It's how you know that you are growing as a person and facing new challenges. A friend once told me, "If it's not scary, it's not interesting." However, it's not okay to allow your fears to prevent you from letting go of the things, jobs, opportunities or people that you no longer prefer to have as part of your life.

Most of the people I meet who feel comfortable discussing the topic tell me that their fears generally break down into two distinct categories:

1. Rejection Fear. This is the fear associated with how others perceive you, the actions you take and/or the things that you stand for. For the majority of us, our natural desire to be accepted by others is so powerful that, when not accepted for whatever reason, we feel we do not measure up. The key to letting go of your rejection banana is to improve your self-image. At the very moment you are so secure in who you are, what you stand for and how you act, you become immune to how others think about you and your fear of rejection disappears. Your responsibility in life is to be the very best person possible, and the moment you allow your fear of how others think of you dominate your life, you have sacrificed your personal power. The best way to overcome the fear of rejection is to work on improving your thoughts and feelings about yourself. Personal growth always reduces the fear of rejection. It's also

important that sometimes another person's thoughts and feelings about you may have nothing to do with who you are or what you stand for as much as it may have to do with the other individual's personal agenda. Some people need to make themselves feel better about who they are by attempting to make someone else feel worse. Be very careful about what you let through the filter in your mind. Not every opinion is worth giving energy to.

2. Consequence Fear. This is the fear associated with what may happen to you if you take certain actions. Think back to when you were in school. The teacher would ask the class a question and giving the answer required raising your hand. Some kids, the ones that knew the answer, raised their hands immediately. Others, without a clue to the answer, would start shrinking behind their desks in the hope that they could some-how become invisible and the teacher would not call on them. Growing up I was always amazed at how the teacher would seem to zero in on me hiding behind the student in front of me, absolutely petrified that I would be called on, not have the right answer and be embarrassed in front of my classmates. That's consequence fear at work; our overwhelming concern that we may fail when doing or being asked to do a certain thing. And when we fail, most of us become embarrassed, so we shy away from actions for fear of how others may perceive us and, as a result, we limit our experiences and diminish the quality of our lives. Remember, most of the things that we learned in life came after a series of failures. You didn't walk the first time you tried to stand as an infant, and you probably weren't a very good driver the first time you got behind the

wheel of your car. It's okay to take chances in life, it's okay if the first time you attempt something you are not as successful as you had hoped. Just stay fully engaged in doing the things that matter most to you and you will overcome your fear of the consequences of your actions.

So the next time you experience the feeling of fear ask yourself, "Where is this coming from?" Is it the fear of personal rejection or the fear of the consequences of your behaviors? Regardless of the source of the fear, you cancel fear with a passion greater than your fear and an improved self-image that makes you so secure in who you are that others cannot intimidate or hurt you.

Living a life free of limiting bananas comes with a price and fighting fear often comes with a big price tag. When you choose to pay that price with the firm belief that beyond your fear there is an opportunity to advance your life, you will be free of things that have held you back.

What You Can Do

❏ Confront fear and make it your friend.

❏ Read self-image building books.

❏ Associate with people who have the qualities that you aspire to possess.

❏ Understand that a little fear can make life exciting.

❏ Be selective about who or what you allow to influence your feelings.

*The things that you
fear the most prevent you
from having the things
that you want the most.*

Make Greatness Your Destiny

I believe that each of us is born with the potential to achieve greatness during our lives. Greatness is your destiny if you are prepared to appreciate that short-term greatness or a lifetime of greatness is a matter of seeking and believing.

You never really know what your personal potential for greatness is until you accept the fact that we all live in a world of limitless opportunities. The fact that you may not be able to see those opportunities from where you are in your life right now does not diminish the fact that they are there. You just have to seek and believe.

Belief is a powerful tool. Holding the belief that you are pre-ordained for a life without barriers or bananas is the foundation upon which you can alter each day of your life and build for a better future. However, merely wanting a better existence is not enough. If wanting were all it took, each of us would have all that we aspire to and desire to possess. Desire is the beginning; creating is the essential. It's what we create that frees us to accomplish more. It's what we believe we deserve that allows us the freedom to engage our most powerful possession—our thoughts.

Belief that there is a better life for you sets you free to use your imagination. And at the very moment you are willing to imagine greatness for yourself, you are on your way to a life without limits. I have always said that all achievement in life begins with the question, "What's possible for me?" When you start to ask yourself questions about your possibilities, you begin the process of letting your imagination run free. Our imagination always exists in image form. Imagination literally means *our images in action.* Seeing yourself fulfilling your destiny for greatness begins with your willingness and ability to visualize a better future. And believing you are worthy and deserving of that better future is how you move one giant step closer to your personal potential. Remember, you were designed for greatness. Believe that with all of your heart and soul and you will be amazed at all of the wonderful people and situations that will appear in your life, almost as if by magic.

Seeking and finding opportunities to create a better destiny exist all around us every day. All we have to do is open our eyes to what's possible and increase our power of awareness. The more you look for opportunities, the more you will find them. Recently, after 10 very demanding days of business travel, I was on the final leg of my trip home. The airplane was in an oversold seat situation and so when the flight attendant asked if there was anyone who wanted to give up his or her seat for another person and receive compensation from the airline, nobody volunteered. However, when the flight attendant made her second announcement looking for a volunteer, she mentioned that the seat was for a soldier on weekend leave who needed to get home to see his family. The people on the airplane volunteered by the bundle. During that moment of kindness and concern for another person, an individual may have fulfilled his or her destiny and achieved greatness.

As a boy, I spent many of my summers at the Catskill Mountains in upstate New York. I loved to go fishing and would do so at every opportunity; but before I could head down to Baileys, I had to find some worms. Without a bait store or the money to buy bait even if there was one, I had to dig for my own worms. Eventually, I learned that if I looked under enough rocks, especially after it rained, worms were abundant. I learned some valuable lifelong lessons looking for worms:

1. If you really want something badly enough, you may have to look under some rocks to find what you want. A big part of experiencing and enjoying greatness is finding and acting on opportunities when they are presented.

2. Achievement usually requires sacrifice. If you want something you must be prepared to pay a price. And the price you pay may be steep and come in many forms.

I said greatness is your destiny; I never said that achieving greatness was always fast, easy or convenient.

I remember when actor Christopher Reeve died. Famous for playing the role of Superman and with numerous other ac-complishments in show business, he was destined for greatness,

I believe. Almost completely paralyzed as the result of a horse-back riding accident, he endured years of painful rehabilitation and managed a relatively remarkable recovery beyond most expectations. He spent nine years wheelchair-bound and during those nine years he continued to direct films, became a spokesman for stem cell research and a powerful advocate and fund raiser for research that hopefully will someday help others recover from spinal cord injuries. I assure you that as a young man or for that matter the day before his accident, he never imagined that his greatness might come as the unintended result of a situation that life handed him.

I guarantee that there have been times in your life when something happened to you that left you totally baffled. I call it a 2 x 4 event. Life is rolling along smoothly and all of a sudden from out of nowhere we feel as if we were hit in the back of the head by a large piece of lumber. When those events occur, you have some choices. You can either be smothered by the situation, in which case

The quality of your life will largely be dependent on the quality of your choices.

you become of little use to yourself or anyone else around you; or you can look beyond the obvious situation and seek the opportunity to grow as a person. It is important to remember that the quality of your life will largely be dependent on the quality of your choices. So, when confronted with the opportunity to shape your destiny, always know for certain that thoughts are things, thoughts create energy, and energy creates outcomes.

We can never know what the future holds in store for us and we may never understand how we arrived at the present condition of our lives. What we do know is that our destiny will largely be driven by our beliefs and behaviors. Armed with that information we can consciously make better choices in our lives. And as a result of those choices increase the likelihood of finding and achieving our destiny. Given complete freedom to think any thought, I encourage you to THINK BIG! It does not require any more mental energy to think bold and limitless thoughts than it does to give energy to the things that prevent you from letting go of small thinking and limited possibilities. It's okay to have outrageous thoughts as long as you understand that to enjoy an extraordinary life, a life free of rotten bananas, you need to be prepared to take outrageous action. Only when you take outrageous actions can you attract into your life outrageous outcomes. So, be courageous and always remember that if you truly believe that you were destined and designed for greatness, opportunities to achieve greatness will come your way. And, when you deliberately seek opportunities to advance your life, those opportunities will appear. Seize those opportunities and make the most of them. When you do you are on your way to the greatness that you so richly desire and deserve.

"A man who stumbles upon the work he was meant to do is destined to become the king of something..." —Thomas Carlyle

Find your passion, and miracles can occur in your life.

What You Can Do

❑ Think big!!!

❑ Remember that greatness is a choice.

❑ Work to improve your awareness of opportunities.

❑ Think of yourself only in the very best of terms.

❑ Embrace the belief that you are worthy of a life filled with unlimited possibilities.

❑ Become the King or Queen of something.

KEY #10

Future Vision

If you want to leave your rotten bananas behind you, it is extremely important to spend the majority of your time, effort and energy on where you are going, rather than where you have been. Because you are only able to think one thought at a time, when you invest your mental energy in your future, you make your past part of your life experience and create the environment for a brighter future. It's okay to reminisce and recall the wonderful experiences of your past. However, whenever you divert your mental energy to those things that were limiting or negative, you run the risk of repeating bad behaviors.

We become what we think about most of the time, and the things that we focus on are likely to become our destiny. Remember, thoughts are things and thoughts have power and energy. So be mindful of your thoughts because what you think about comes about. That means that you literally have to discipline yourself to monitor your thoughts as well as the words that you use to express your thoughts and feelings. Your words are a direct reflection of the quality of your thoughts and will

105

always reflect the quality of your mental attitude. To effectively shed the past and dramatically improve the quality of every aspect of your life going forward, you must spend the majority in the moment and the remainder of your time on your future. Basically, all we have is NOW. In order for us to enjoy all of the good things in life, we must be appreciative of what we have and recognize that each moment of life is a gift that can be taken away from us at any moment. That reality is not designed to alarm or depress you; its purpose is to make certain that you divide your mental energy between what you have and what you can prepare for in the future. And, while sometimes our lives are filled with surprises, some more positive than others, for the most part when it comes to designing your future, you get experience from what you focus the majority of your energy on.

Because our words trigger our visual images and our visual images trigger our thoughts, the more we actively concentrate on what we want and the less we cling to the things that are not working in our lives, the closer we move to achieving a more gratifying life. So condition yourself to pay more attention to what you invest your mental energy in and watch your words—they are the mirrors of your thoughts. The more you focus on what

> *You need to see your future in your mind's eye before you can ever live in the reality of your vision.*

you want and only what you want, the more you will notice how much more fun life becomes. It's a case of mind over matter and mind over mouth. If it's not important, don't focus your mental energy on it; and if it's not worth mentioning, keep your mouth shut.

It has taken me years to discipline myself to not say some of the things that run through my mind. I have learned that when it comes to personal and professional success, people are far more impressed with the things that I do than by what I say. And the more I have learned to become the master of my thoughts, the easier my life has become. The key is to stay in the moment and enjoy it for what it offers—and plan like crazy for your future. After all, the future is where you will be spending the rest of your life. And as you plan, remember the old expression, "Man plans and God laughs." When it comes to the future, some things are just beyond our ability to understand or control. There are times when you just have to ride out the storm, hold on tight and maintain the belief that everything that takes place in your life is either designed to teach you a lesson or strengthen you for the challenges of the future.

In order for you to create a new and better vision for life and achieve FutureVision, you must spend a little bit of time each day mentally rehearsing your desired results. In other words, you need to see your future in your mind's eye before you can ever live in the reality of your vision. The willingness to envision what you want for yourself on a daily basis is essential if you want to dramatically alter your life for the better. Life is perceptual, an illusion, a creation of our imagination or simply buying into the beliefs of how others think we should be. What we see in our own existence others may see entirely differently. Your limitless ability to create a new vision for your life by using your powers of visualization will astonish you. And, nothing on earth will make your dreams come true more than the belief that you deserve the things that you desire.

Once you come to the realization that your thoughts and imagination have the power to alter your destiny, you are armed with a very powerful weapon. Change your mind and you can change your life. Change what you see in your mind and you change your destiny. If you are dedicated to incorporating FutureVision into your life, tomorrow is like an unwritten newspaper. You get to determine your future and create a new reality for yourself. And at the very moment you can see and imagine a better future for yourself, you have taken a giant step toward personal growth and a life without limitations.

As a child, I never imagined in my wildest dreams that I could live the life I have come to enjoy. I believed that some people were just blessed and lucky, that their destiny was shaped by others or by some grand plan beyond their control. As I came to understand the ability of the mind to latch onto a vision and belief and make it my reality, I felt as if I possessed some magical power. The power to see my future in my mind and make that vision my reality was freeing.

One day while driving through a very affluent area of New York looking for a place to build a home, I came across a magnificent piece of property. Located on the gold coast of Long Island, it was all that I ever hoped for in a place to live. When I tracked down the real estate broker who represented the property, I was stunned by the asking price. It was more than double what I had saved for a parcel of land and seemed beyond my ability to attain. To make matters worse, the broker told me that the seller would not accept any terms and wanted to be paid in cash. For weeks all I thought about was that land

and how much I wanted to live there. I visualized a beautiful contemporary home surrounded by magnificent trees, with a swimming pool in the back yard and a tennis court. The idea of living there consumed my free time and when I had nothing else to do, I would drive to the property and stand outside my car visualizing the home of my dreams nestled in the trees. Of course I had no clue that this could eventually become my reality, I just knew with great clarity exactly what I wanted.

A clear vision remains the genius of all creation and all you have to do is get crystal clear about your wants, then trust that the "how" will take care of itself. I believe that the things in life that you want, want you. And so it was that one evening while sitting at home watching television, I tuned in to a made-for-television movie called "A Whale for the Killing." It was the story of a man whose sailboat was wrecked in a storm, leaving him and his family stranded in a whaling village while waiting for his boat to be repaired. As he waited, a whale became stranded in a lagoon. The big news in the village was that the whalers, who had not had much success lately, finally had an opportunity to kill the whale and generate much-needed income by selling its oil. The thought of killing the whale was such an unimaginable idea to the man who was stranded that he and his family launched a very unpopular campaign to save the whale. Needless to say he was met with tremendous resistance

When it comes to altering your personal and professional destiny, a clear vision coupled with a large dose of passion about what you want will serve you well.

109

from the townspeople. The more they wanted to kill the whale, the more determined and committed he was to save the whale. As the story unfolded I was moved by his determination. I was inspired by his dedication to a principle and how much he believed that he could defy great odds and change the course of the villagers' lives and save the whale.

When it comes to altering your personal and professional destiny, a clear vision coupled with a large dose of passion about what you want will serve you well. When you have more faith than fear, you can change your life for the better. More determined than ever before to own that property, I called the real estate broker and asked that she set up a meeting between the seller and me. I was told that the seller rarely met with potential buyers and would not negotiate the price of the property. In spite of the broker's warning, I insisted on and finally got the meeting that I had requested, and it went perfectly. The seller was so moved by my vision of the house that would sit on the property that he sold me the land on the spot and even negotiated the price. When I faced the situation, I had a choice. I could give in and find all kinds of excuses why things didn't work out to my advantage or I could lock onto my vision, focus my energy, call upon my resourcefulness and proceed as if I could not fail.

When you are clear about what you want and all of the steps necessary to arrive at your destination, and then totally invest all of your mental and physical energy in your future and the attainment of your goals, you tip the odds of success in your favor.

Remember, when it comes to your future, you get to choose or you can let others choose for you. I strongly recommend that you take complete control of your life and work to make your FutureVision your reality. Know for certain that you have a limitless ability to visualize a better life for yourself. Believe that the more you lock onto that vision and imagine yourself as having all that you think about and see in your mind's eye, the more your life improves. Then, keep your vision clear in your mind and never hesitate moving in the direction of what you want. Remember, taking responsibility for your destiny is the highest level of all personal growth and achievement, and when you accept that responsibility for yourself and act boldly, you change your future.

A good question to ask yourself when it comes to your future is: "If I were not living my present life, what would my new life look like?" When you can answer that question and visualize what that new life looks like in vivid detail, your powers of a limitless mind will become more fully engaged. Then if you take the time to write down precisely what your new life looks like and focus on that image on a daily basis, you will find yourself presented with the necessary opportunities to dramatically alter your destiny. Almost as if by magic, wonderful things will happen to and for you as your future begins to reflect the things you focus your mental energy on.

Then the only thing that remains to be done is to trust someone who you believe will act as your personal support system as you work on your future. This individual should be someone who you can use as a sounding board and who will encourage you to achieve your personal greatness. This person will never judge your vision and motives unless they believe that you have chosen the wrong path, in which case they will challenge your direction in order to make sure that you are acting out of clarity and total commitment. This partner in persistence is your cheerleader, moral compass and future coach all rolled into one caring, trustworthy and truthful person.

Remember, very few people in life can achieve greatness on their own. Life change tends to be a team effort, and the more people you have encouraging you, the more you will be inclined to take the steps necessary to craft a better, brighter future for yourself.

What You Can Do

❏ Focus only on what you *really* want.

❏ Vividly imagine yourself living the life of your dreams.

❏ Put your FutureVision on paper. Remember, if it's not in writing, it doesn't exist.

❏ Sell your vision to at least one important person in your life.

❏ Think of yourself as totally deserving of the life you see yourself living.

❏ Never hesitate to act on opportunities when they present themselves.

❏ Remain purposeful, passionate and persuasive.

Nothing has any meaning beyond the meaning you give it.

The Habits of Heroes

I have always believed that what others have done, you can do. Your ability to look at and study the achievements of others will act as an inspiration for your own personal accomplishments. At the instant you view and admire another person's greatness, you can use that image as the catalyst for your own success. And while each person's success story can often differ in many ways, there are some habits, behaviors, traits and characteristics that most of your heroes possess.

If you are truly committed to living a life without rotten bananas, I suggest that you study, embrace and then emulate the actions of others who have achieved personal or professional success in their lives. The success of the people you have read about or who have greatly influenced your life in a positive way should serve as the role models upon which you launch a life without limitations. Their success stories should serve as your inspiration and continually remind you of what can be accomplished when you put your heart and mind to work. These heroes have learned the lessons of ridding themselves of the rotten bananas in their lives on their way to greatness. As with most things, when it comes to designing your future you will be met with choices and, to the extent that you choose wisely, you will win!

So, here are some of the habits I believe will support you in your quest for the best that life has to offer:

1. *A high sense of priorities.* Taking the time to organize your life and having a clear sense of personal and professional priorities is essential if you want to enjoy a brighter future. Because it is impossible to focus your energy on more than one thing at a time, you need to have great clarity about what is really important to you and what is not. I recommend that you start each day with a list of things that need to be accomplished and then work your list by achieving each task and making certain that you focus on the tasks which influence your life in the most beneficial ways. The more you work your list and the clearer you are about what's important to you, the more you will experience a sense of accomplishment. Achieving is a habit. When you are in the habit of doing and accomplishing all that can be done each day, and when you consistently work in the direction of your dreams, the closer you come to being a hero.

2. *Clarity of vision.* Your mental picture of what your life will look like when you shed all of your limitations must be crystal clear in your mind. The more vivid the picture, the more you engage your power of attraction. As you add detail to your vision and lock on to those details, you will move closer to a life that reflects what you see it to be, rather than what

116

it has been in the past. That's why it is so important that you know precisely what you want and pour all of your creativity and imagination into refining that image.

Heroes in all areas of life always engage the power of their minds in order to see the end result in advance of it happening. Remember, vision creates reality. And, it's not so much what your vision is, as it is how your vision changes the way you think and act that matters most when it comes to getting what you want. Your mind works in pictures, not words. Your words are for creating images. Limitless people know that the only thing that really matters is the quality of the outcomes in their lives. They spend so much time focusing on the eventual end result of their vision and actions that they never have time to imagine anything less than what they want. So, when you have visual clarity and a high degree of certainty about what you aspire to become, you are on your way to a banana-free existence.

3. *Personal resilience.* If you are truly committed to achieving greatness in any area of your life you must realize that anything worth having is sometimes worth fighting for; and you are going to lose a few fights along the way. I have never met anyone who achieved all that they had accomplished without some personal or professional setbacks as they moved in the direction of their desires. Expect some valleys as you go, and do the things that people with heroic behaviors do. They get up one more time than they are knocked down. Their "never-give-up and never-give-in" attitudes prevail in their minds and are exhibited in their behaviors. By becoming more resilient and going with the flow of life on a habitual basis, they determine their own destiny. When you adopt a realistic approach to the

hills and valleys of life, you will be happier and live a life that is more fulfilling and less frustrating. Just make sure that you are always moving in the direction of what you want.

4. *The habit of doing more.* So much of personal achievement has to do with your ability to look at a situation and critically evaluate it for what it really is. Most of the things that happen to us in life provide us with an opportunity to maximize our potential. Some people go through life looking to do the very least possible and others do whatever needs to be done…and then some! I am certain that you have been presented with opportunities to merely complete a task or go beyond the expected and strive for perfection. When you look at what you have done, ask yourself, "Have I achieved all that is possible?" Then do whatever remains to be done, and you will have adopted an important habit of all heroes. By doing all that you can each day—as close to 100% as possible—you will accomplish more and feel a very powerful and positive sense of achievement. Remember, highly meaningful action will create a more meaningful future. Stay busy, stay productive and get the most out of yourself and each day of your life.

5. *A strong feeling of self.* Heroes understand that they cannot create a life that is greater than what they deserve. That's why people who want to live a life without limitations spend so much of their free time working on improving themselves. Here is the key: spend more time working on growing yourself than you do on either growing your business or any aspect of your personal life. Success in life follows self-image and, unfortunately, so does failure. To the extent that you embrace the

habit of lifelong learning and personal self-improvement, you will improve all of the opportunities you are faced with in life. And when you act on those opportunities, you move closer to greatness and a life that is free of constraints. Remember, you can only build a life up to the limits of your self-image, and the more you work on improving how you feel about yourself and what you are deserving of, the more success you will have in your life.

6. *Renegade thoughts and behavior.* Eventually you need to come to grips with how much of what you do has to do with the opinions of others. If you live your life thinking the thoughts that someone wants you to think and behaving as others would have you behave, you have surrendered your personal freedom to someone else. In order to get rid of the limitations of your past you must be willing to think and act on a totally different level. Living your life to please others never seems to work in the long run. You will become stagnant as a person and resentful of the life that you have been saddled with. Your most powerful possession is the ability to think extraordinary thoughts and then take bold actions that bring you closer to what you want for yourself. Heroes in life spend the majority of their time thinking and acting beyond the expectations of others. They have a strong feeling of self, are never afraid to go against conventional thinking, and have come to understand that, for the most part, if everyone is doing the same thing in the same way, there is probably a better way. When you accept the responsibility to improve your thinking and act on those new and improved thoughts, your behaviors will change and so will the outcomes in your life.

7. *Dream unrealistic dreams.* Heroes know that an active imagination can overcome all barriers. They are willing to forget how things get done, and remain crystal clear about what needs to be done. Once you are certain about what you want, you will be presented with opportunities that provide you with the "how." Remember, all barriers are self-imposed and mostly a product of your imagination. The more you focus your mind on what you want and how you are going to get it, the less mental energy there is available to think limiting thoughts.

"The proper function of man is to live, not to exist."
—Jack London

If anyone has ever told you to keep your dreams and aspirations realistic, remember, the code word for realistic is "low." The question you want to ask yourself is: "If I had no limitations, what could I accomplish?" When your dreams are limitless in scope and when you can see yourself in your own dream, you change your life for the better. You were designed for greatness...never settle.

8. *An attitude of invincibility.* Heroes know that the shortest distance from where they are to where they want to be is the space between their ears. There mindset is one of invincibility; they just believe that they can and will accomplish whatever they have set their minds on. Their vivid imaginations allow them to see the invisible and achieve what others consider impossible. They know that most limitations are based on fear, so they continually move in the direction of their desires in spite of what others may say or think.

When your personal passion for a better life becomes greater than your willingness to settle for the life you are presently living, you will become invincible. Regardless of the bananas, obstacles or barriers that you confront, you will find a way to reign victorious.

Perhaps one of the best examples of how you can become a hero of change and get rid of the limiting bananas of your life is the Etch-A-Sketch™ toy of your youth. Etch-A-Sketch™ was a self-contained, red framed plastic container with a screen on which you could draw images by turning a couple of knobs. When you were done or wanted to eliminate what you had drawn, you would vigorously shake the toy and the images would disappear. It's a good example of what you need to do when you want to change your life. Take a good, hard look at what you have and, if you don't like what you see, shake things up. You get to create a new vision as often as you are unwilling to accept some of the limiting pictures in your life.

The heroes of the world are not necessarily special people. For the most part they are just like you and me. They simply go through life believing that they are deserving of more and are willing to do whatever it takes to live a better life. They are unafraid of taking chances and are willing to live with the consequences of their decisions. As highly decisive and thoroughly determined individuals, they are fearless in the face of adversity and never accept the status quo as their destiny. They know that altered behavior is the link between where they are and where they want to be. And they also know that in life people are either advancing or receding in their lives.

You are never in neutral. You adopt the habit of heroes when you choose to continually and consistently advance in the direction of your dreams, shedding all of the things that have held you back.

What You Can Do

❏ Create a list of your priorities.

❏ Shake up your life whenever necessary.

❏ Keep your goals high.

❏ Work harder on yourself than anything else in your life.

❏ Be unafraid to go against conventional wisdom.

❏ Do whatever it takes to become a hero to yourself and others.

❏ Adopt the habit of personal persistence.

*Competency can happen
in a moment.*

Building a Better Bunch

I n life, you mostly get what you deserve, not necessarily what you want. If wanting was all it took to have a more enriching life, then I suppose each and every one of us would have all that we ever desired. I am hoping that at this point in the book you know exactly how important your self-worth is and feel more deserving of a better life for yourself. You have come to the realization that you were designed for greatness and a life without limitations, as you break the shackles of your past. You will always have some bananas in your life. The key is to rapidly identify the ones worth keeping and the ones that are rotten. Building a better bunch is a product of heightened awareness and rapid action.

It's time for you take charge and become the Chief Executive Officer of your own life. When you accept the responsibility of being your CEO, you become empowered to govern your thoughts and actions and take total and complete control of your future. You get to decide what bananas to shed and which ones will serve you well as you advance in the direction of your desires. You have come to understand that assigning the condition of your life to other people or outside forces is a waste of time, effort and energy. You appreciate that your past may have been chosen for you, but you get to choose the rest of your life. That is a very powerful feeling and when you allow that feeling to become the foundation of your emotions, all that you think about and all of the actions that you take will allow you to grow in every aspect of your life.

Here are some guidelines for you to consider as you become the CEO of you and take charge of the rest of your life:

1. Think one step ahead and always have a back-up plan for whatever you are doing; don't put all of your plans in one basket. Life is filled with surprises and from time to time you will be faced with barriers or obstacles. For the truly creative and resourceful, an obstacle is something that you can work your way around. However, if you are faced with an immovable barrier, rather than investing your time and energy into dealing with something you may not be able to overcome, resort to your back-up plan. Remember, challenges in life can strengthen your resolve and build your character, so be flexible when the situation calls for resilience and steadfast when an obstacle is in your path.

2. Understand and effectively utilize the power of your personal affirmations and self-talk. The two most important words of personal power are "I am." When you think and speak in terms of "I am," you will become! Because people think about 4-5 times faster than they can speak, it's important to improve

the quality of your thoughts about yourself more than anything else. For the most part, what goes on between your ears is a lot more important than what comes out of your mouth. Your mind is like a magnet and the things you think about the most are the things that will appear in your life eventually—both positive and negative.

Personal affirmation is the key to altering your outcomes. How you view your world, your work, your life, your relationships and yourself are a matter of personal choice. Your goal is to continually reinforce positive thoughts and feelings about yourself. To evolve you must consistently remind yourself of what you need to be doing and redefine how you do those things. You must mentally rehearse how the rest of your life is going to be in advance of those improvements occurring and believe with all of your heart that the things your aspire to will become your reality.

3. Be childlike in your unwillingness to accept "no" as an answer. Children are incredibly persistent; and until we as adults bombard their brains with a series of "no's", they will do whatever it takes to get whatever they want. Those of you with children know exactly what I am speaking about. Kids just want what they want and they usually don't give in until they get it. Be like that! Most times a "no" means nothing more than "not now." So be deliberate about what you want and when confronted with a "no", dig in and totally invest yourself in the attainment of your goals. As the CEO of you, you will find that there is absolutely no substitute for persistence and the belief that you are worthy of a life without limitations. Remember, there is always a way to get what you want out of life if you are really committed to getting it.

4. Live the principles of T.E.L.L.—Teaching, Earning, Laughing and Learning. When you spend a portion of your daily life teaching others how to improve their lives, you improve your life. When you work toward earning a monetary living as well as earning the admiration and respect of others, you improve your life. When you take the time to enjoy the lighter side of life, you enrich your life. And when you invest yourself in a program of lifelong learning, the personal growth that you are sure to experience will impact everything you do for the rest of your life. Be sure to incorporate the principles of T.E.L.L. into your everyday life and you are certain to rid yourself of the rotten bananas of your past.

5. Always deliver more than you promise. When you live up to your word and then give more of yourself than even expected, you elevate yourself and how others view you. Doing what needs to be done, doing it in a timely manner and as close to perfection as possible is a habit that, once attained, will provide you with more opportunities in life as well as build your personal confidence. At the conclusion of dinner one evening at a fine New York restaurant, I ordered Bananas Foster for dessert. When the beautifully prepared dessert arrived, I happened to notice that my Bananas Foster had absolutely no bananas. You would think that bananas would be the primary ingredient and I was amazed that they served me the dessert. They served me "Foster," no bananas. When I asked the server about the missing bananas, she indicated that the kitchen was out of bananas and if I wanted she would deduct the cost of a banana from the bill. Amazing! That was my last time at that restaurant! To enrich your life you must

always strive to deliver more than expected and attempt to never disappoint.

6. When given the choice on how to think and behave, always choose limitless over limited. It's a simple choice. When it comes to your personal potential, you pretty much get in your life what you set in your mind. Remember to spend the majority of your time and energy looking where you are heading in your life. Beyond your limiting bananas lies a world of unbelievable opportunity, adventure and greatness. You will eventually be defined by how you identify yourself, and when you think in limitless terms, you expand your potential. Always keep in mind that we live our lives in a world of pictures and when it comes to improving your future, the only things that really matter are the images in your mind. That's why you should spend considerable time doing visualization exercises and have a place where you can post the images of everything that you envision for yourself. Only imagine the very best for yourself and only see yourself as a person without borders or limits. Try this…make a mental movie of just how the rest of your life is going to play out. The more crisp the images in the movie of your mind, the more likely you are to live the image you have created.

7. With a dramatic need for speed, decide to break the speed barrier for changing your life. As long as you have chosen a life without limits, the faster you move in the direction of your goals, the better. If rapid change makes you uncomfortable, just remember that comfort is not necessarily your friend. If you are too comfortable, you probably aren't taking

very many chances or maximizing how fast you can change your life. Your mission is to consciously and actively seek discomfort, remembering that comfort comes from repeating past behaviors. Those behaviors are linked to the habits of your past. Remember, you can change your life in an instant if you are willing to live more on the edge and put urgency behind all of your decisions. Decide what needs to be changed, change it with a positive expectation and change it fast. You get to go as fast as you want and, with the clock of life always advancing, the faster you let go and get going, the better.

8.   Become more purposeful in your thoughts, actions and attitudes. Since we are all moved by our motives, when you effectively manage your motives and approach your life with great clarity of personal purpose, life becomes more fun and you expand as a person. People are like businesses in that they are never neutral in movement. You are either looking to give or looking to gain and, for most of us, if we are not gaining, we are groaning. When you give more than you get, you grow. You are either advancing or declining as a person and if you cannot demonstrate how you are advancing, you are in a state of decline. Remaining in a state of sameness is never an option and will keep you clinging to the rotten bananas of your life. When you bring more to the party of life than you take away, you free yourself to find the greatness you desire and deserve. Remember, each and every day of your life you have the privilege of dancing with your destiny. You are either sitting the dance out or you are up and moving. To live a more meaningful life, there is no substitute for purity of purpose.

9. Eliminate the 8th day of the week: "Someday." Letting go of your bananas is a **now** thing. All too often I meet people who live their lives regretting not having changed their life sooner. Even worse, too many people live lives of quiet desperation and never improve their lives at all. They just plain settle. Letting go of your bad bananas must take place **now,** not later. By procrastinating and putting off until Someday the things that need to be done, you restrict your growth and diminish your personal potential. If some personal or professional relationships need to be changed, do it **now.** Remember, the quality of your life is usually measured by the quality of your relationships. So, if you need to make a change and let go of someone that is not an advocate for your success, the sooner you cut that person loose, the better. When you choose immediacy over putting things off, the quality of life will change about as fast as you do.

With the clock of life continually running, can you really afford to wait? There will never be a better time to strive for excellence in your life. Remember, where excellence exists, no excuses are required. So do what the winners in life do. Decide **now** to change whatever needs to be changed in order to make life better. And, live your life in the **now** with all of the energy and passion that you have and plan your life as if you will live forever, leaving no detail to chance.

What You Can Do

❏ **Work on your relationships. All personal growth is relationship driven.**

❏ **Maintain a need for speed and decide what you need to do NOW.**

❏ **Stay clear about your purpose in life.**

❏ **Only imagine the very best for yourself.**

❏ **Take emotional ownership of everything that you do and always do what's right.**

❏ **Follow your instincts; you already know exactly what you want your future to be.**

The best way to change tomorrow is to take care of today!

FINAL REMINDERS ABOUT
Banana-Free Living

1 While this may be painful to accept, you may represent the rotten banana in someone else's life. If so, be prepared to do whatever it takes to change and move forward with your life. Sometimes the best thing another person can do for you is to set you free to find your happiness elsewhere. Then, take a good hard look at who you really are, how you think and behave, and then make whatever changes are necessary to make yourself the ideal "you."

2 Remember, very few things in life are forever and a great many things in life are not always what they initially appear to be. A rotten banana today can become a better banana tomorrow. And what may appear as a life filled with beautiful bananas today may turn rotten in the future. In order for you to maximize what is possible for you in your life, you must be flexible in your attitudes and practical in your actions. If you want the life you believe you are entitled to, you must work to remain as optimistic as possible.

3 To advance beyond your present place, you must think beyond your present thoughts and see yourself beyond your present state. Your subconscious mind always accepts your desires as attainable and always responds with a "yes" to the things that you truly want. Remember that the past is a place of reference, not residence; and the reason the windshield is larger than the rear view mirror is because you are supposed to spend more time looking forward than backwards. So, make certain that you only define yourself on how you will be when you advance beyond your present place.

4 Personal and professional greatness is often defined by your imagination. Remember, bottlenecks are always at the top of the bottle and so much of what we experience in our lives is a result of what takes place in our minds. Beyond the obvious lies the possibility of an amazing future, and when you totally invest your mental energy in a life beyond the one that you are living and can see your future clearly in your imagination, your visions will become part of your reality. An active imagination can overcome all barriers.

5 Belief is a powerful tool and the more you are willing to step outside of your current beliefs about any limitations that you may have, the closer you are to a life of limitless possibilities. Your creative mind has the ability to envision the life of your dreams. So, stay focused on your personal serenity and focus on the quality of choices that you make each day. Freedom to believe that you deserve a life without rotten bananas will energize and empower you to get more enjoyment out of life.

6 The future is where you are going to spend the rest of your life and the best way to insure a brighter future is to plan long-term and live in the "now." After all, the present is all that we care really count on. As it is said, "It's called the 'present' because each moment is truly a gift"; cherish it. Because so much in life depends on personal accountability, your number one task is to function in the "now" and plan for the future. Remember, your subconscious mind accepts your visions and beliefs as true and attainable.

7 To improve what you get out of life you must be prepared to think different thoughts, take different actions and consistently work on your level of deservedness. The more you believe yourself worthy of a better life, the more you will have a better life. It's your self-talk that shapes your self-image and all personal improvement is self-image based. Passion and desire drive greatness, and when you direct all of your mental energy, physical efforts and emotional enthusiasm in the direction of your goals—and do so with passion—the quality of your life improves. Remember that the best reason for personal and professional excellence today is the promise of a better life tomorrow.

8 Understand that there is a big difference between motivation and willpower. Motivation tends to be an outside thing that temporarily alters the way we think, feel or act. Unfortunately, if you rely on motivation to improve your life, you will always be reliant on outside forces. However, when you have willpower, your energy is internally driven and your level of personal inspiration will keep you moving in the

direction of your desires. Remember, willpower tends to be driven by a strong sense of purpose. When you are clear about what you want and stay focused on a greater purpose, you will find the necessary resources to work wonders in your life.

9 Letting go of the status quo is very often the end result of no longer accepting and tolerating the present condition of your life. Your ability to change your viewpoint about yourself and your potential is your most valuable possession. When it comes to what is possible for you in life, there are no barriers, only erroneous beliefs. To a great extent, someone else created many of your beliefs about who you are as a person and what your personal potential is. What if they were wrong? To go beyond where you are, you must first think and behave beyond who you are. And while your past may have been predetermined, your future remains unwritten. At the moment that you are willing to alter your beliefs and behavior, your barriers will come crashing down and your rotten bananas will disappear. Follow your instincts…you already know what you want.

10 Reinforce your personal uniqueness on a daily basis. The things that make you special will become the foundation of your self-worth. You cannot create a life that is greater than what you believe you deserve, and the quality of your life will always mirror your feelings of self-worth. Never overlook your personal accomplishments or personal qualities. So often we focus on what's missing at the expense of what we have already achieved. A better life begins when your positive vision of yourself is matched by your courage, your work ethic and your preparation.

11 Decide to really focus on the quality of your decisions. Ultimately, the quality of your life will be in direct proportion to the quality of your decisions. Very often, the only thing that keeps the rotten bananas in your life will be your decision to allow your current condition to continue. When you make better decisions, you will live a better life. And the decisions that you make today will eventually determine your tomorrow. The only way to improve your future is to control your present, and your decisions are the foundation upon which your future rests.

12 Be bright, resourceful and aware of what it takes to rid yourself of limits as you pursue your life without limits. Here is a rule that I suggest you follow when you want to improve your life, a rule that has worked for me and I am confident it will work for you:

When you have more time than money, use your time.
When you have more money than time, use your money.

Each of us has experienced and lived through some defining moments in our lives. When confronted with events that rock you to your very core, understand that these events will never leave you exactly the same. You will either be weakened or diminished in who you are or enlivened and strengthened as a person. Remember, your next greatest challenge could be cleverly disguised as your next greatest opportunity for growth. Stay totally committed to getting the very most out of life as you let go of your bananas and enjoy a life without limits.

NOTES